The Shadow of Death

(90-Day Journal-Devotional from 9/11)

ARLENE + SHERM
BARNS

PRAISE THE LORD

Rev Cletus J. Balder

BookLocker.com, Inc.
2011

First Edition

The Shadow of Death

(90-Day Journal-Devotional from 9/11)

Chaplain P. L. Holder

DEDICATION

This book is written to honor, to offer heartfelt respect and true appreciation to, all who helped one another and a whole city traverse through the Valley of the Shadow of Death experienced during the 9/11 timeframe.

A special note for those of the various military branches who served, suffered and struggled during 9/11, written by one who was there as part of the support team and one who still deals with a heavy heart every year as September 11th arrives and memories are awakened. I recognize many today continue to suffer from and struggle with their memories of events about their time at 9/11. Therefore, I have combined snippets of the news for the day combined with personal experiences and writings I completed while in New York City along with some newly composed prayers, poems, and various illustrations to offer words of hope, assurance and encouragement. *Chaplain (LTC) Patrick L. Holder – Retired*

Table of Contents

ACKNOWLEDGMENTS

I am grateful for service with the active Army, Army Reserve and National Guard for more than forty years. These years enticed me to consider writing many stories and devotionals about military life. My first consideration comes from my New York City - 9/11 experiences.

I thank my God who has been my ever present source of inner strength.

I am lovingly grateful to my wife, who has supported me, during many times of separation to complete over 40 years military service within the Active Army, Reserve and National Guard.

I also thank my daughter, Joy Holder, who is a photographer for the Senate in Washington, D.C. She presented a quote that struck home and spurred me toward listening to God's prompting. "God is my author, writing my story within many other stories." *(Joy - 31 Aug 09).*

My prayer is God's blessing upon all who read this that you may be lifted knowing that no matter where we are or what we are doing, God is there.

My thanks to the many friends who have encouraged me to proceed along with the many clergy and laity who have previewed sections of the writings and offered personal support, guidance and some needed correction?

Special recognition goes to the following Web sites which confirmed and reminded me of several historical occasions that merit mention to include Biblical resources along with a special thanks to my editor who spent several hours reviewing and revising as needed.

1. The White House – President George W. Bush http://georgewbush-whitehouse.archives.gov/index.html
2. September 11 News.com
http://www.september11news.com/Sept11History.htm
3. Sermoncentral.com/illustrations
4. Crosswalk.com *Chuck Swindoll's Day by Day Devotional*
5. Scripture verses are from Biblegateway.com with quotes from: 21st Century King James (KJ21), American Standard Bible (ASB), Amplified Bible (AMP), Common English Bible (CEB), Contemporary English Version (CEV), Darby Translation (DARBY), Douay-Rheims 1899 American Edition (DRA) English Standard Version (ESV), God's Word Translation (GW), Good News Translation (GNT), Holman Christian Standard Bible (HCSB), King James Version (KJV), The Message (MSG), New American Standard (NASB), New Century Version (NCV), New International Readers Version (NIRV), New International Version (NIV), New International Version 1984 (NIV1984), New International Version UK (NIVUK), New King James Version (NKJV), New Living Translation (NLT), Todays New International

Version (TNIV), Worldwide English (New Testament) (WE), Wycliff Bible (WYC), Young's Literal Translation (YLT).

6. Editing services provided by: *Shadra L. Bruce, writer and editor follow me @shadra blog: IGotMomPower follow @gotmompower.*

Chapter 1

Introduction

"THE LORD is my Shepherd [to feed, guide, and shield me], ...though I walk through the [deep, sunless] Valley of **The Shadow of Death**, I will fear or dread no evil for You are with me; Your rod [to protect] and Your staff [to guide], they comfort me." *(Psalm 23:1a, 4 (Amplified Bible))*

Chuck Swindoll prayed: "Father, if those people we know who have trudged through the valley of the shadow of death were not alive today, walking with You and telling us to keep going, where would we be? How much we need their examples and encouragement! Thank You for

"The great faith that led our nation's Founding Fathers to pursue this bold experience in self-government has sustained us in uncertain and perilous times; it has given us strength and inspiration to this very day. Like them, we do very well to recall our "firm reliance on the protection of Divine Providence," to give thanks for the freedom and prosperity this nation enjoys, and to pray for continued help and guidance from our wise and loving Creator."   —George H. W. Bush, May 3, 1990

each one." (**"Day by Day,"** *Charles Swindoll, July 2005, Thomas Nelson, Inc., Nashville, Tennessee.)*

Praise the Lord for all the people with whom I met and served during the 9/11 experience. The Lord is my personal shepherd, and I am writing from my call to active duty, daily events and personal experiences as a military chaplain, knowing that many words have been said that are very profound when it comes to facing the Valley of Death events of 9/11, events that, to this day, leave a shadow of death in our minds and hearts. The Scriptures, needless to say, were my basic source of inspiration as I approached the events of 9/11.

My dates of service in connection with 9/11 were: 11 September 2001 – 3 February 2002 and 1 – 10 April 2002.

Where were you on the morning of 9/11 2001? This is a simple question which most of us can answer because it was a day of lasting impressions even when you think of it years later. What were you doing when you first heard or saw the news of that fateful morning?

It started as any other day at my house. I had gotten up, dressed and taken my granddaughter to school. I then drove to the dry cleaners to drop off my National Guard fatigues to be cleaned and pressed. As I was turning them in, I watched their TV, which was showing a plane flying into a tower, and I stated: "that looks interesting." I asked, "What movie is this?" The attendant then informed me that this was not a movie but had just really happened in New York City.

After I regained my thoughts, I commented, "I might be back to pick up those fatigues!" I left, turning my car radio on, which I seldom listened to. I went back to my office, and at 10 am I received a call to report to duty at my unit, which was located 30 miles from New York City, before the end of the day. Several hours later I was there.

An evening formation was called, everyone's current role was explained and tasks were assigned. The Chapel was opened and made available for anyone who so desired.

The next day, I connected with the Command Sergeant Major (CSM) and Executive Officer (XO) and headed into New York City to personally assess the situation and determine any further missions our unit might have.

Upon arrival at Ground Zero, both the Executive Officer (XO) and the Command Sergeant Major (CSM) tried to enter the impact zone to evaluate our future responsibility for security and support but were denied access, so we walked the perimeter.

However, Praise the Lord, **The Power of the Cross** was pre-eminent, because when I, as the chaplain, later requested access, it was granted and they allowed the CSM and XO to accompany me.

Late Wednesday afternoon (Sept. 12th) I was able to clearly identify that the devastation was massive; the rubble was unbelievable, the stench was horrific, and the atmosphere was heavily mixed with enormous sorrow. The thinly visible air was filled with a cloud of dust, debris and whatever. The work zone was easily recognizable but possessed an eerie silence amidst all that was going on. The smoke was still rolling from the twisted steel as firefighters continued to work the hot spots. Rescue workers were slowly sifting through the rubble. We walked the area seeing the shadow of death all around us. Our job was to determine the points of security providing relieve for local police, enabling them to continue to protect the rest of the city, which by the next day command had in place.

There were so many who came to help from so many places: firemen and women, dog handlers, FEMA personnel, construction workers, heavy equipment operators, medical personnel, and food service workers. They quickly provided such a variety of services from job-specific tasks to simply handing out water.

A make-shift morgue had already been established as bodies were being removed and identified. The deaths were already weighing heavy on those who worked there. Tragically, as we entered the morgue, an infant's remains were being brought in to be identified.

We entered to see if there was anything we could do to help. The FEMA chaplain came over, identified himself and said he was there and we would need to leave. We honored his request, and I said to myself, "Praise the Lord." He was there and included as a valuable part of the medical team.

After what seemed like hours, my crew headed away from the shadow of death with a plan of action in place. We returned to our unit and tried to sleep, knowing what was coming next.

My job, as unit chaplain, was to be advisor to the commander, counselor for those in need and worship leader for the military community. My responsibility, within New York City, was to make an every-other-evening trip to the city to visit the service members who were stationed throughout the perimeter of the Impact Zone. I was serving as their counselor, comforter, encourager, or simply their friend, since the military presence was not welcomed by all. There did end up being some interesting cases during my months of duty within the city, some, of which will be included, within these writings, while others will remain a memory, by request of those involved.

Think about those first few days: "Where did you first go to worship, pray, gather, or console yourself or others when the events of 9/11 happened? Do you remember? How did you deal with the news of the event in your own life, or are you still years later dealing with it?

The first chance I got, Thursday the 13th, I went to the Post chapel, where I had an office and temporary sleeping quarters, and we gathered for prayer. Needless to say, I had a full house, as many churches, synagogues and other places of worship did. I led in the 23rd Psalm to remind the people that we do have a Savior, a Shepherd, who truly does care for us. Then I offered the following prayer:

"Tragedy struck as many arose that fateful morning during September. We need to begin anew helping those who suffered loss when family, friends and so many perished. Lord, how do we as a Christian society cope with this sorrow? Let us daily pray God's blessing upon Soldiers, Marines, Sailors, Coast Guards and Airmen now serving. Help them to be safe from harm. Protect until battles have ceased. Please take care lifting each anxious moment, showing great love. Listen, everyone, to God. Witness special glory and become blessed. Then, offer praise for the strength to handle each personal challenge and help us encourage and strengthen one another. Amen."

As activities progressed, part of my responsibilities included providing daily devotionals, which sometimes overlapped into a couple of days depending on the evening's events in the city, plus my weekend responsibilities back at my church in Elmira, New York. These WORD devotions were posted, in a power-point frame with the acronym and a scripture verse, throughout the compound to encourage, inspire and strengthen our service members during their experiences in the shadow of death. My desire and prayer was, with God's help, I would hear the right words and be able to share them.

Mark Twain said, "The difference between the almost right word and the right word is really a large matter–it's the difference between the lightning bug and the lightning."

The shadow of death was a new experience for many within the command, although there were some combat veterans. But even those who had been there and done that expressed how this event was so different because this happened in their country, on their homeland, and for many, in their city and their home. Many of the unit members had lost someone. This shadow of death was surreal, scary and for many; quite intimidating.

Therefore, I wrote "The Word" for the day, developed mostly from the initial prayer that I read on the 13th. I would use a word from that prayer as an acronym, either writing a poem, prayer or other form of thought. I will use these words as we join for a daily historical and personal journal with devotional tour through 9/11.

Prayer: "Yours, O Lord, is the greatness and the power and the glory and the majesty and the splendor, for everything in heaven and earth is yours. Yours, O Lord, is the kingdom; you are exalted as head over all." *1 Chronicles 29:11 (NIV)* Amen.

Chapter 2
Terror Was Experienced (1-7)

"Tragedy struck as many arose that fateful morning during September."

"We do not war primarily with races as such. Tyranny is our foe, whatever trappings or disguise it wears, whatever language it speaks, be it external or internal, we must forever be on our guard, ever mobilized, ever vigilant, always ready to spring at its throat. In all this, we march together. Not only do we march and strive shoulder to shoulder at this moment under the fire of the enemy on the fields of war or in the air, but also in those realms of thought which are consecrated to the rights and the dignity of man.......Let us rise to the full level of our duty and of our opportunity, and let us thank God for the spiritual rewards He has granted for all forms of valiant and faithful service." – *Winston Churchill, Monday 6 September 1943*

T.R.A.G.E.D.Y Struck - *I shall not lack – Psalm 23:1b*

"**Sept. 12:** New York Mayor Rudolph Giuliani warns death toll will be in the thousands at the trade center. Firefighters continue to douse flames in New York and Washington. Bush labels attacks 'acts of war' and asks Congress to devote $20 billion to help rebuild and recover." *September11News.com*

"Finally, be strong in the Lord and in his mighty power. Put on the full armor of God so that you can take your stand against the devil's schemes." *Ephesians 6:10-11*

A whole day has almost completed; dust was still thick in the air and great sorrow was in the silence as military and civilian forces joined to work through and win over this tragedy. Many rescuers had already put in a double-day's work while the military finalized security procedures surrounding the site.

The first devotional, and many others, was written as a poem. This one is entitled T.R.A.D.E.G.Y:

- **T**o our surprise evil arose in our land

- **R**esulting in many dead at their hand.

- **A**nger quickly arose within our land,

- **G**et even has become the ongoing demand.

- **E**veryone's hope is rebounding in our stand.

- **D**ecisions have been made by military command,

- **Y**ou remove this evil from our land.

"You and I have within ourselves the resources for achieving amazing things if we do not allow our problems to overwhelm us. You may know the story of a young Hungarian athlete in the 1952 Olympics who won a gold medal with his ability to shoot a pistol. His right hand and eye coordination were so perfect that he simply could not miss the bull's eye. Six months later that young man lost his right arm. Such a tragedy would have overwhelmed many of us. It did not overwhelm this young man. Four years later at the Melbourne Olympics he was back and he did it again. Another gold medal. This time he shot with his left hand. We have in us the ability to turn tragedies into triumphs-- or, in Schuller's words, to turn scars into stars." – *Unknown (Sermon Central.com/Illustrations).*

"And that about wraps it up. God is strong, and he wants you strong. So take everything the Master has set out for you, well-made weapons of the best materials. And put them to use so you will be able to stand up to everything the Devil throws your way. This is no afternoon athletic contest that we'll walk away from and forget about in a couple of hours. This is for keeps, a life-or-death fight to the finish against the Devil and all his angels.

Be prepared. You're up against far more than you can handle on your own. Take all the help you can get, every weapon God has issued, so that when it's all over but the shouting you'll still be on your feet. Truth, righteousness, peace, faith, and salvation are more than words. Learn how to apply them. You'll need them throughout your life. God's Word is an indispensable weapon. In the same way, prayer is essential in this ongoing warfare. Pray hard and long. Pray for your brothers and sisters. Keep your eyes open. Keep each other's spirits up so that no one falls behind or drops out." *(Ephesians 6:10-18 – Message Paraphrase MSG)*

Prayer: Lord, let us remember on this 9/11 and each to come, not the long hours, the devastating loss of property and life, or the uncertain future. Help us remember; "Even though I walk through the Valley of the Shadow of Death I will fear no evil for You are with me, Your rod and Your staff, they comfort me." *Psalm 23:4 (NIV).* For this we are grateful O Lord! Amen.

S.T.R.U.C.K. Down

"**Sept. 13**: Fighting back tears, Bush vows that America will 'lead the world to victory' over terrorism in a struggle he termed the first war of the 21st century." *September11News.com*

"Therefore humble yourselves under the mighty hand of God, that He may exalt you in due time, casting all your care upon Him, for He cares for you." *1 Peter 5:6-7 NIV*

Winston Churchill proclaimed: "Death and sorrow will be the companions of our journey; hardship our garment; constancy and valor our only shield. We must be united, we must be undaunted, and we must be inflexible."

Two days, few in numbers so far, but they seemed more like a year each. Time creaked along with long hours and much exhaustion. People would greet you on the street with open conversation about their personal comments concerning 9/11. There was so much confusion, fear, misunderstanding, destruction, and the list goes on. So many people came up and asked "Chaplain, why?" There were no real answers at that time and maybe none yet today for some.

The one "why" I heard the most was: "Why them and not me?" This question was often followed by thoughts that should have been joyful; however, the thoughts were full of sorrow, thoughts like:

1. I was part way there and realized I left some important papers at home and went back for them.

2. I missed the train I usually take to work!

3. I got stuck in traffic, and then I heard on the radio and simply broke down and cried.

   Sorrow has fully filled the air,

   Trauma has affected everyone.

   Reality says this act is not fair,

   Understand this act was in bright sun,

Causing death – they did not care,

Knowing many are hurting everywhere.

4. I was just getting ready to walk into the building when I heard and saw what happened.

5. I had to take my kids to school and therefore I was late for work.

Looking back we know the times life trickles along. We may choose to let it control us, or we can learn to adapt, thanking God for each day, each new breath, facing tomorrow knowing God has promised grace sufficient for each new day and trial.

Over the many years of service I have learned of survival with God's protection. He has been my personal guard and shield (besides driving in New York City) in Vietnam, Desert Storm, a near fatal car accident, and heart surgery. I have no doubt; God is in charge and not me, and I am very grateful.

Prayer: Let us reflect on the words of President Andrew Jackson: "Finally, it is my fervent prayer to that Almighty Being... that He will so overrule all my intentions and actions and inspire the hearts of my fellow citizens that we may be preserved from dangers of all kinds and continue forever a united happy people." Amen.

M.A.N.Y. Affected

"**Sept. 14**: Bush declares national emergency and gives military authority to call 50,000 reservists to active duty...Bush leads four former presidents and nation in prayer at National Cathedral and visits trade center." *September11News.com*

Many more were affected, as the news of the day verifies.

"...let us consider one another in order to stir up love and good works, not forsaking the assembling of ourselves together, as *is* the manner of some, but exhorting *one another,* and so much the more as you see the Day approaching." *Hebrews 10:24-26 (NKJV)*

"God is able to make a way out of no way and transform dark yesterdays into bright tomorrows. This is our hope for becoming better men and women. This is our mandate for seeking to make a better world." *Martin Luther King, Jr.*

Without question 9/11 affected many people both within the city and from states throughout the U.S. I emotionally united with and spoke to many people dealing with heavy hearts and troubled souls – people who struggled and snuggled, slept on cots in vacated hotels and the pews of open churches daily. All to bring about a calming assurance that life is valuable and loss is a difficult reality.

Many in New York City with strained, aching, and burdened bodies tirelessly labored, some in total silence to find – the living – the lost and to secure remains.

- A mighty force has gathered to date,

- Supporting the city during its trouble.

- Men and women from many a state,

- Arrived to pitch in during this struggle.

- Now our people have united to relate,

- Yes – people are even willing to snuggle.

It was great to see there was no thought of race or creed, no discussion of beliefs, simply strangers working together to accomplish an almost impossible task of intermingled searching, identifying, and hoping. The hard work, the daunting hours, the places to eat, the places to rest – the work continued around the clock. Yes, many were affected – to include those who never touched foot on the concrete and tar of a big city before.

> Charles Kendal Adams tells us: "No one ever attains very eminent success by simply doing what is required of him; it is the amount and excellence of what is over and above the required that determines greatness."

A nation arose September 11th and joined with those at Ground Zero, connected to this terrible tragedy whether from our desk, kitchens, workshops or in our cars. We listened to the radio, watched the TV and asked many questions. What did you do when you arose? In the city they:

- **A**ll together worked side by side

- **R**eached out to neighbors all around.

- **O**pened arms continued to abide

- **S**miles helped remove the frowns.

- **E**veryone was trying to continue in stride.

Prayer: Lord, I humbly pray Your Word: "…, I do not consider myself yet to have taken hold of it. But one thing I do: Forgetting what is behind and straining toward what is ahead, I press on toward the goal to win the prize for which God has called me heavenward in Christ Jesus. *(Philippians 3:13-14 NIV)* Amen.

T.H.A.T. F.A.T.E.F.U.L. Morning

"**Sept 15:** Abroad: Pakistan agrees to the full list of U.S. demands for a possible attack on neighboring Afghanistan." *September11News.com*

What was being thought about as necessary and important at home differed from the realities within the city – death, life, shelter, safety, a home, job, personal fears and victories, and you probably can add your own thoughts that differ.

"I am leaving you with a gift"- peace of mind and heart. And the peace I give is a gift the world cannot give. So don't be troubled or afraid. *John 14:27 NLV*

Charles Spurgeon writes, "It is the most bitter of all afflictions to be led to fear that there is no help for us in God."

As 9/11 annually approaches, what do you think about? I think about **T.H.A.T.** day often and the many days since, where I worked along with so many in the ruins of the city. As I worked on my devotion one day the word was **T.H.A.T.** I realized how some had grown so much in such a short time re-evaluating their personal frailty.

- Think about how you have grown.

- Have you seen a change in your life?

- All this tragedy has made you moan.

- Then turn to God with your strife.

How has it affected you as an individual? Are you able to accept the truth of what John wrote? "... Don't be troubled or afraid." *John 14:27 NLV*

Prayer: Heavenly Father, we pray knowing **F**rom the beginning of time mankind has **A**ttempted to rule the earth without **T**alking to you. Help us develop an **E**very-day life that inspires us to **F**aithfully – individually – personally call **U**pon You for strength, hope and **L**ove that reaches out and embraces those around us.

Therefore, help us to: "Seek God while He's here to be found, pray to Him while He's close at hand. *(Isaiah 55:6 Message Paraphrase)* in order that we, as Your created representatives, might learn the peace that comes from knowing Your heavenly family, Father, Son and Holy Spirit. Amen.

Good M.O.R.N.I.N.G.

"**Sept. 16:** "Two other airplanes were flying near the hijacked United Airlines jet when it crashed in Somerset County, but neither had anything to do with the airliner's fate," the FBI said yesterday.

In fact, one of the planes, a Fairchild Falcon 20 business jet, was directed to the crash site to help rescuers. "There was a hole in the ground -- that was it," said Yates Caldwell, the pilot who was at the controls of the 10-passenger corporate jet for Greensboro, N.C.

The voice recorder would have picked up the last 30 minutes of conversation in the cockpit, unless the hijackers turned it off or it was too severely damaged in the crash. It was found around 8:25 p.m. Thursday, 25 feet below the ground in the crater gouged out by the doomed jet." *(Sunday, September 16, 2001 By Bill Heltzel and Tom Gibb, Post-Gazette Staff Writers)*

"This is the day the Lord has made, we will rejoice and be glad in it" *Psalm 118:24 (NKJV)*

"The gloom of the world is but a shadow. Beyond it, yet within easy reach, is joy. There is radiance and glory in the darkness, could we but see, and to see, we have only to look. I beseech you to look. Life is so generous a giver, but we, judging its gifts by their covering, cast them away as ugly, or heavy, or hard. Remove the covering, and you will find beneath it a living splendor, woven of love, by wisdom, with power... Everything we call a trial, a sorrow or a duty, believe me... the gift is there and the wonder of an overshadowing presence. Our joys too: be not content with them as joys. They, too, conceal diviner gifts." *- Fra Giovanni, 1513*

One **M.O.R.N.I.N.G. during September** many were lost and some were found. However, I am not talking about the bodies, but the souls that were lost that day. Think about it: one morning during September, all those who went to eternity, ready or not.

I have always enjoyed the quote (author unknown) that asked: "Are you a person who says Good Morning Lord or do you say, Good Lord – It's Morning." I enjoy saying "Good Morning" even when I was working in New York City, because each day was a new chance to meet someone new, help someone with a different situation, pray for a special need, comfort a struggling soul, or simply listen to a troubled voice. What is this morning to you?

- **M**ay this, for you, be a day to start anew?

- **O**pen your heart and receive God's love.

- **R**each out and take what God has for you.

- **N**ever forget all the resources from above.

- **I** want you to realize that God has a plan

- **N**ot for the evil one to win over man.

- **G**od desires all to respond to his demand.

Prayer: God, some days it is so difficult to get started and to say Good Morning, Lord. The burdens of the family, job and health never seem to end. As I look at these tragedies, help me not only see the enemy at work. Help me also see Your Presence, Strength and Love continually there to provide and powerful undergirding support. Lord, provide the light to guide me through the shadows that still linger. Amen.

D.U.R.I.N.G. Recovery

"**Sept. 17:** The supreme leader of Afghanistan's hard-line Taliban says a grand council of Islamic clerics will decide whether to hand over bin Laden. The Federal Reserve cuts its key interest rate to try to keep the economy from plunging into a recession. Investors send stocks reeling on Wall Street's first day of trading since the attacks. The list of people FBI wants detained in the United States and abroad grows to nearly 200." *September11News.com*

"I will exalt you, LORD, for you rescued me. You refused to let my enemies triumph over me. O LORD my God, I cried to you for help, and you restored my health." *Psalm 30:1-2 NLV*

Larry Moody, who teaches a Bible study class on the PGA Golf Tour, told Paul Azinger, who found out he had cancer: "Zinger, we're not in the land of the living going to the land of the dying. We're in the land of the dying trying to get to the land of the living."

God works in so many ways that confound and confuse, often without us understanding how. Daily you and I face many new events. Some affect us and others are just news. What do we do during the times that we are affected? What do you do during the recurring time frame of 9/11? Does it still grip you with fear, or confusion, or lethargy, or does it cause you to search your own soul? Does it bring you into a chilling shadow of uncertainty striving to find the light of hope?

We are able to recover and walk through the shadow. Recovery is the process that we respond to in individual ways. Some need strong medicines, while some need to relearn how to function. Some heal quickly, while others need more time. Some never heal until eternity. Have you recovered from the hurts of 9/11? Think about this:

- **D**ay by day the Lord abides with

- **U**s, providing, giving, loving, everyone.

- **R**eady is He to meet our personal wishes,

- **I**nspired to draw us close to His Son.

- **N**ow is the day He is calling for you

- **G**ive yourself that you may know what has begun.

Prayer: "… I tell you, now is the time of God's favor, now is the day of salvation."*(2 Corinthians 6:2 NIV).* Now is the time, since we have no idea what our next morning may be like or if that day will give us time to recover. Lord, remind us that if we are ready it will not make a difference. In Your Name I Pray. Amen.

One Morning in S.E.P.T.E.M.B.E.R.

"**Sept. 18:** Taliban leaders call on Muslims to wage holy war on America if it attacks. U.S. Defense Secretary Donald Rumsfeld says administration preparing sustained offensive against terrorists and countries that support them. Bush leads nation in moment of silence." *September11News.com*

"So always be ready, because you don't know the day or the hour the Son of Man will come." *Matthew 25:13 NCV*

September 11th, 2001 was a simple and sorrowful reminder of how short our days may be with no warning when they may end.

- Salvation is readily yours and mine.

- Each one looks at it differently since that day.

- Please, lord, let Your light brightly shine

- Through faithful people in a wonderful way.

- Entrust Your wisdom to all who believe,

- Many desire, right now, to receive.

- Be our source of guidance as we travel along

- Encourage each to find their individual song.

- **R**eward with wisdom that outwits the wrong.

"Sometimes I find myself like the little boy reasoned in his prayer to God. He told God that 'Lord, if you can't make me a better boy, don't worry about it. I'm having a real good time like I am.' We get so caught up in realizing accomplishments that we see rewards of our efforts that are only temporary." – *Unknown*

God's desire during September, or any other month, is that we choose to look for, work for, encourage for, and instruct for others the idea of living daily in His wisdom with the knowledge that our greatest reward is eternal.

Prayer: Praise You, Heavenly Father for each day and each opportunity to enjoy all You bring our way. Instruct, mold, prepare each of us that we may represent You in all that we do. Thank You for this opportunity and challenge. **Amen.**

Chapter 3

Response Was Offered (8-9)

"We need to begin anew"

Abraham Lincoln, 16th President of the United States: "We have been recipients of the choicest bounties of Heaven. We have been preserved these many years, in peace and prosperity. We have grown in numbers, wealth and power as no other nation has ever grown; but we have forgotten God. Intoxicated with unbroken success is the necessity of redeeming and preserving grace, too proud to pray to the God that made us. It behooves us, then to humble ourselves before the offended Power to confess our national sins and to pray for clemency and forgiveness." *(Abraham Lincoln, Proclamation of a National Day of Fasting and Prayer, March 30, 1863, Washington, D.C.)*

W.E. N.E.E.D. T.O.!

"**Sept 19:**   Beamer, of Cranbury, N.J., died Tuesday aboard United Airlines Flight 93, which crashed in Somerset County. Before the crash, Beamer dialed zero on the onboard phone system, reaching an operator at GTE in Chicago. He told her the plane had been hijacked.

Jefferson, a supervisor at GTE, got on the line and talked with Beamer for 13 minutes, telling him about other hijackings that had ended in crashes at the World Trade Center in New York.

Beamer told Jefferson he and other passengers planned to take on the hijackers. He made Jefferson promise to call his wife, Lisa, and sons David, 3, and Andrew, 1.

The last words Jefferson heard from Beamer were to his fellow passengers: "Are you guys ready? Let's roll."

Minutes later, the plane crashed, short of its presumed target of Washington, D.C., the last of four crashes in a span of about an hour.

No one aboard survived the crash, but authorities believe the passengers' actions prevented much greater carnage." (*Wednesday, September 19, 2001 By Jim McKinnon, Post-Gazette Staff Writer*)

"Arise, LORD! Lift up your hand, O God. Do not forget the helpless." *Psalm 10:12 (NIV)*

"Everything can be taken from a man but one thing: the last of the human freedoms – to choose one's attitude in any given set of circumstances, to choose one's own way." – *Viktor Frankl*

We need to! Do what, you may ask? Those on the plane in Pennsylvania made their decision about what they needed to do. In

New York City, everyone was doing their best to be in their place doing their thing trying to bring it all together. What was it we needed?

We look back recognizing what we had, the many avenues of support.

Worship was provided by a multiplicity of clergy in churches, parking lots, outside buildings, small rooms and the great outdoors.

Engineers worked around the clock to make it a safe place to do search and rescue, remove material safely, and check for structural integrity.

Nurses dutifully and tirelessly worked in emergency rooms, morgues, worksites and wherever requested to provide services. Usually they were bearing a tearful smile with unusual strength in their eyes. They were an outer support for a hurting society.

Educators, civilian and military, combined forces and were offering courses in Critical Incident Stress Debriefing (CISD) to enable anyone who was having difficulty dealing with their feelings and emotions in regard to the events of 9/11. They were making CISD available long after the events had passed.

Enterprising civilians opened their restaurants, set up water stations, made sandwiches, and cleaned floors and bathrooms.

Doctors of many types put their skills to work. There were medical doctors, chiropractors, massage therapists, acupuncturists, physiatrists, psychologists, dentist and probably some doctors I knew nothing about. These specialists provided their services freely for those who were in the rescue, cleanup and security forces.

Timely supporters: Many street vendors and individuals worked at churches and restaurants to provide food, resting places, quietness, and fellowship

Organizers: I offer a special thanks to the skilled, talented and well-functioning work of the FEMA crews, Red Cross, Search and Rescue crews – to include the specially-trained dogs, military and civilian security, plus all other groups that kept things flowing in a steady direction toward mission accomplishment.

Prayer: Heavenly Father, we join together in giving thanks for all who have come together to help in the time of need. Be with all who journeyed the second mile while dealing with their own personal issues, emotional struggles and spiritual battles during their time of specialized aide. God's blessings upon each endeavor past and present. Amen.

B.E.G.I.N. A.N.E.W.

Sept. 20: At the joint session of Congress, President Bush said, "We have seen the state of our union in the endurance of rescuers working past exhaustion. We've seen the unfurling of flags, the lighting of candles, and the giving of blood, the saying of prayers in English, Hebrew and Arabic. We have seen the decency of a loving and giving people who have made the grief of strangers their own. My fellow citizens, for the last nine days, the entire world has seen for itself the state of our union, and it is strong.

Tonight, we are a country awakened to danger and called to defend freedom. Our grief has turned to anger and anger to resolution. Whether we bring our enemies to justice or bring justice to our enemies, justice will be done."

"If we confess our sins he is faithful and just to forgive us of all unrighteousness." *1 John 1:9 (NIV)*

Service members were all in place, each doing their assigned task. Each day was the start of a new 24-hour time frame and a time to begin anew if needed. Think of the many within New York City, some who were now serving their country, who had to start over after the 9/11 tragedy. Some were still hoping and looking for some sign of a lost loved one, others were searching for a new home or job, and still others were not sure what they were searching for but knew they had not found it yet. They searched amidst the clouds of gray ash, the rubble of destroyed buildings, and the faces of those at the outskirts of the work zone. Looking!

Many, in their personal lives, were searching and had to start life all over because of an error in judgment, an improper attitude, an accident or a recognized need that it was time to change.

They had to begin anew! They had to begin anew, especially when they looked at the variety of mistakes they had made, the things they had said, the friends they had offended, and the sins they had committed. Their past experience versed their present life. Are you in a place where you need to begin anew?

For some involved in the 9/11 experience, September 11th will always be a turning point, a reminder that they had to start over anew celebrated the fact God had given them another chance.

"Imagine a sponge that has been used to wash the dishes. It's all full of dirt and food and old water. It needs to be filled with clean water! But how can you do that? Easy, you wring it out, rinse it off, and wring it out again. Only when you have done this can you fill it with clean water.

It's the same with the Spirit (of God). Here we are, all full of sin and grime and filth. There is no room for Him. But once all the filth has been removed, and we have been emptied, the Spirit can come and fill us anew." – *Unknown (Sermoncentral.com/illustrations)*

"Every tomorrow has two handles. We can take hold of it with the handle of anxiety or the handle of faith." – *Henry Ward Beecher*

- **B**oy, how many times I have wanted to begin,

- **E**rasing the mistakes of my past.

- **G**ive me victory over my ongoing errors and sin

- **I**nspire me to stay faithful till the last.

- **N**ow – not tomorrow – help me receive His best.

Writing today I respond by saying:

Another day, lies before us, with 24 hours to pass.

Never knowing what will be our individual fate.

Each day a new opportunity, in our life, will pass.

Wonder – how will you and I will relate?

"I know that there is nothing better for people than to be happy and to do good while they live. That each of them may eat and drink, and find satisfaction in all their toil—this is the gift of God." *Ecclesiastes 3:12-13 (NIV)*

A. N.E.W. beginning occurred at 9/11 for many a person. However, there were those who had difficulty starting anew. How about you?

Prayer: Lord, help us

Announce to the world how much you truly care

Never questioning the Holy Spirit's power we share

Enriching us with glorious wonderful strength anew

Winning because we walk holding hands with You.

'Lord we thank You because we know "…those who wait on the LORD shall renew their strength; they shall mount up with wings like eagles, they shall run and not be weary, they shall walk and not faint. Amen.' *Isaiah 40:31 (NKJV)*

Chapter 4

Acknowledgement Was Experienced (10-20)

"Helping those who suffered loss when family, friends and so many perished."

President Harry S. Truman stated: "Let us all stand together as Americans. Let us stand together with all men everywhere who believe in human liberty. Peace is precious to us. It is the way of life we strive for with all the strength and wisdom we possess. But more precious than peace are freedom and justice. We will fight, if fight we must, to keep our freedom and to prevent justice from being destroyed. These are the things that give meaning to our lives, and which we acknowledge to be greater than ourselves….this is our cause: peace, freedom, justice. We will pursue this cause with determination and humility, asking divine guidance that in all we do we may follow the will of God."

The Dog's Room – A H.E.L.P.I.N.G Hand

"**Sept. 25:** The President called for a helping hand. The United States and six of the world's richest nations agree to produce a coordinated plan to freeze the assets of all terrorist organizations. Saudi Arabia cuts ties with the Taliban government. Osama bin Laden's organization makes a fresh call to arms, saying 'wherever there are Americans and Jews, they will be targeted.' The Pentagon calls nearly 2,000 more reservists to active duty, bringing to 14,318 the number of Reserve and National Guard members called so far." *September11News.com*

The dust was starting to subside when the requests started coming in from city personnel who had been displaced from unsafe buildings. One of the soldiers in my company was tasked with being a helping hand for a woman whose only family was her dog. She had left with her little dog in hand but was missing some of his personal supplies. The soldier was asked to return to the apartment and retrieve certain particulars, an easy mission completed with success. However, that evening the soldier wished to speak to me. He was feeling great that he could help someone in their time of need but a little frustrated due to the fact he also had lost his home because of 9/11 and was now living on an army cot. He knew he would have to start over. But that was not his real frustration as further conversation revealed. He was actually upset that the dog had a better home, with much more valuable possessions, than he did. We had fun discussing this!

We sometimes are called upon to be a helping hand challenging our own position in life, whether it is at home or on the mission field. Let the experience become an adventure.

"He (God) has delivered us from such a deadly peril, and He will deliver us again. On Him we have set our hope that He will continue to deliver us." *2 Corinthians 1:10 (NIV)*

Today remember we have an outstretched hand that is always ready to help us in any way necessary, be it in riches or poverty, greatness or humility, certainty or uncertainty or unknown shadows that linger.

Help is always available, for each of us is true.

Everyday Your Love does protect and provide.

Long-term care is always readily available with You.

Plans You direct give us strength to not turn aside.

Inspire us to help individuals battle along with You anew.

Needing and knowing on the winning side we abide.

Grace abundant from You is our everlasting foundational glue.

A **H.E.L.P.I.N.G.** hand is available during our times of tragedy, our times of triumph, our times of lost-ness, our times of searching and even in our times of insecurity. He wants to help if we will let Him.

Prayer: Lord, I thank You for always being there, even when I was where I should not have been or during times when I was jealous of how You had blessed someone else. Lord, I may not always see your presence, but help me to be reminded You are working through those whom I meet along this pathway, those who offer a helping hand, especially in my times of need. Again, thanks for all Your help. Amen.

T.H.O.S.E. Around Us

"Sept. 26: U.S. and Pakistani officials end two days of talks in Islamabad, with Pakistani leaders saying nations agree on military preparations for combating bin Laden's terrorist network in Afghanistan. Thousands, storm abandoned U.S. Embassy compound in Afghan capital of Kabul. United Nations agency says assault on Afghanistan could send up to 1.5 million refugees into Pakistan and other neighboring countries." *September11News.com*

"Let everything that has breath praise the LORD. Praise the LORD." *Psalm 150:6 (NIV)*

Those around us do affect who we are and what we do as we in turn affect them. One day while traveling through Grand Central Station, one of my soldiers told me to be careful what we said as we went through one of the archways. I asked him why, with all these people here and the boisterous racket, I am lucky to hear you? He told me that there were places where, if you whispered, it could be heard on the other side of the arch. I said, "you have got to be kidding; in the midst of all this noise?" Thereupon, he proceeded to show me how it worked by walking over to the arch, telling me to cross the room and listen on the other side. I heard him as clear I heard him when I was standing next to him. I was amazed. It made me think about all those people, some right next door, who do not hear the person standing next to them. We forget that God hears us when we are talking directly to him and when we whisper; in the light of day or the shadows of life.

Look at all **T.H.O.S.E.** people around you. Do they appear to be lonely and looking for answers, when too often they are not even sure what the questions are? Are you looking for comfort while wanting to comfort others, looking for peace and joy which seems to evade you as well as them?

There remained in the midst of all this love and support, the homeless in their cardboard homes, easily identified as I travel around the perimeter visiting my service members. There are those dressed in shabby clothes and those dressed in clothes that would take a pastor's annual salary to afford. The diversity is seen throughout the city; we see the people – but do we truly?

Mother Teresea stated: "We have drugs for people with diseases like leprosy. But these drugs do not treat the main problem, the disease of being unwanted. That's what my sisters hope to provide. The sick and poor suffer even more from rejection than material want. Loneliness and the feeling of being unwanted is the most terrible poverty."

Lord, today we humbly come before you, in <u>word and *song*</u>, to say help us not only see but also hear **T.H.O.S.E.** around us:

Thank You Lord for Saving My Soul, and to celebrate

How with You *Our Hope is Built on Nothing Less*, now

Open *My Eyes* that I might see the glimpses of truth you have for me.

Search *Me O God* and see if there be any wicked way in me. Then we can rejoice knowing

Everyday *With Jesus is Sweeter Than The Day Before*.

Prayer: Lord, we need You to truly open our eyes to see those not so obvious: the hurting, the needy, the troubled, and the searching, as well as the challenges You bring before us, even within the safety of our own home town. Let us proclaim the songs of our hearts by the way we show Your love. Amen.

W.H.O.M. Do You Trust

"**Sept. 27:** Bush announces plan to bolster airline security, including expanded use of federal marshals on airliners. At Bush's urging, governors around the nation plan to use the National Guard troops for airport security." *September11News.com*

The elements of fear and mistrust were sensed throughout the duration of the cleanup from 9/11. It was seen in the many places of security, checkpoints and inspections of vehicles, at Ground Zero and many of the military installations. Sometimes I could feel the sting of fear from the shadow of death's strong presence as I talked with a service member or worker.

Bridges were constantly being checked; tunnels were watched at both ends and strange events were investigated. There was deep continual suspicion and many still unanswered questions that continued the air of distrust. Service members and civilians alike admitted.

Be reminded that President Bush had said, "On September the 11th, enemies of freedom committed an act of war against our country. Americans have known wars, but for the past 136 years they have been wars on foreign soil, except for one Sunday in 1941. Americans have known the casualties of war, but not at the center of a great city on a peaceful morning. Americans have known surprise attacks, but never before on thousands of civilians. All of this was brought upon us in a single day, and night fell on a different world, a world where freedom itself is under attack." *President Bush – 20 Sept 01 – Joint Session of Congress*

A different world now secured in a different location to add to the many already in existence. I visited each of those airports within proximity of New York City, and spoke with these service members. There was definitely considerable concern about whom they could trust. The air remained infectious with suspicion during this time of coverage. I had even gotten to the point of scrutinizing individuals I saw come in with a suitcase or briefcase. I usually trust people until they proved me wrong. However, the influence of the situation caused me to question: who is that person or whom do we stop and ask to search more thoroughly?

"Trust the past to God's mercy, the present to God's love and the future to God's providence." — *Augustine*

Today I wonder whom do you trust, and are you one to be trusted?

Will you do the work to which you are called?

His plan for you is one that will never end.

Open up to your place in God – do not be appalled.

Mind Him for help against all the enemy does send.

Prayer: Lord, help us to once again learn to trust starting with You, working outward toward our community, county, state and country. Let us recognize that kind of trust which can only come about as we place complete confidence in the simple fact: You are the one in charge. Help us to guard the precious, struggling, suffering, fearful, people whom You place in our lives that they find help, hope and healing. May we be genuine instruments of blessing to those in need and help us identify Your sincere blessings in those whom you place around us. Thank you precious Lord and Savior. Amen.

S.U.F.F.E.R.E.D. In Life

"**Oct. 1:** U.S. President George W. Bush says $6 million in assets are blocked and 50 bank accounts frozen as countries join the U.S. effort to stop the flow of money to terrorist networks. The anti-Taliban alliance in northern Afghanistan and the former Afghan king agree to convene an emergency council as a first step toward forming a new government. The Taliban say the effort will fail." *September11News.com*

Be diligent to present yourself approved to God, a worker who does not need to be ashamed, rightly dividing the word of truth. *2 Timothy 2:15 (NKJV)*

Regrettably, with terrorist acts as well as with war, there are those who suffer or continue to suffer as they look up, look back and even look ahead of the time of terror. One of the saddest nights for me that cause continual caustic memories was September 12th. My mind returns to the death and destruction that surrounded the morgue. I vividly remember the skeletal remains of a young child being brought in. I think about the process of establishing identity and uniting remains with family. The long, heavy, taxing, difficult and wearing process of identification, notification, comforting, counseling and follow up that comes in support of such a tragedy.

Because of that, many would disagree with the statement that what we have **S.U.F.F.E.R.E.D.** in life helps us grow, mature, and become a better person. It is true that scriptures tell us things like: "...we also glory in tribulations, knowing that tribulation produces perseverance; and perseverance, character; and character, hope." *Romans 5:3-4 (NKJV)*

This passage refers to our personal faith, our trust level in God, our ability to recognize that God is in control even though He seems nowhere to be seen.

Does all this suffering help us in living, or does it show us how much God loves us? In this case I agree with Mother Theresa: "I know God will not give me anything I can't handle. I just wish that He didn't trust me so much."

As I was growing up, I heard with frequency from my parents concerning their rationale for disciplining me when I would do something wrong, which seemed to occur with some frequency: "This is for your own good." I did not believe it at the time, since my parents believed in relatively strict disciplining. My grandfather used to sit in a rocking chair, and above that chair he had a leather strap with a motto written above it: "I need thee every hour." Dad had a tendency to agree with Grandpa's idea.

However, as I have become older and wiser and have gone through many periods of suffering. I can also look back recognizing the good I had learned. As our country now looks back at 9/11, are we reminded about what have we learned or have we developed shadows over our eyes, walking with blinders on to hide the memories?

The word S.U.F.F.E.R.E.D. had great significance after 9/11 and continues to have a strong significance today.

- **S**earch the Scriptures for the real truth about your life.

- **U**nderstand God's Word to battle whatever comes your way.

- **F**ind the answers to all the needs found within your life.

- **F**ulfillment is available for the challenges of the day.

- **E**njoyment is available for the ups and downs of your life.

- **R**ewards are continually waiting, God wants to say.

- **E**ternity is the special destination and only one true way.

- **D**eliverance is the goal God wants you to have in your life.

Prayer: Heavenly Father, guide each of us toward diligence in the service that we provide – be it as a member of the military or civilian. Let our service be one of support and encouragement for those who have suffered with a strong dose of the hymn refrain: *"To God Be The Glory, Great Things He Has Done"* even in the midst of struggle, the shadows of life and the uncertainties of tomorrow. Amen.

L.O.S.S. Continues

"**Oct. 2:** NATO secretary-general says United States has provided its 18 NATO allies with "clear and compelling" evidence of Osama bin Laden's involvement in the attacks. Fires continue to burn at the World Trade Center site." *September11News.com*

"But whatever was to my profit I now consider loss for the sake of Christ. What is more, I consider everything a loss compared to the surpassing greatness of knowing Christ Jesus my Lord, for whose sake I have lost all things. I consider them rubbish that I may gain Christ." *Philippians 3:7-8 (NIV)*

People stood outside the restricted area looking in. Some were curious gawkers, some were searching and hoping with their eyes to see some reminder of a family member or friend, some silently expressing grief and some of the workers taking a much needed break looking at the still massive project ahead.

There was one group where members openly expressed themselves. They were the home owners, landlords and tenants who could see their homes and apartments, but due to safety reasons, they were unable to live in or remove anything from their homes. Many were understandably asking "When am I going to get to go home to stay?"

The loss, of property, friends, family and hope was somewhat unbearable, indescribable and unappreciated. Many questioned their ability to be able to recover. There was considerable introspection, soul searching and questioning with little in the line of consolation. The loss of so many people I found to be the hardest question, because I continued to wonder: were they ready to meet their Creator? A horrible act completed brought about the loss of much property and claimed so very many souls. My question was and is: did those who lost their lives gain eternity as a reward or damnation? Because all who died went to their final home to stay!

- **L**ead us to follow the correct path – A straight and narrow path. *(Matthew 7:13-14)*

- **O**pen the doors along the way. – "Behold I Stand at the door and knock." *(Revelations 3:10)*

- **S**upply Your Love not Your Wrath. – "Earth is the Lords and fullness thereof." *(Psalm 24:1)*

- **S**trengthen us without delay. – Everyone who asks receives. *(Matthew 7:7)*

Lisa Beamer reflects on the loss of her husband in her book, *Let's Roll.* "Slowly I began to understand that the plans God has for us don't just include 'good things,' but the whole array of human events. The 'prospering' he talks about in the book of Jeremiah is often the outcome of a 'bad' event. I remember my mom saying that many people look for miracles – things that in their human minds 'fix' a difficult situation. Many miracles, however, are not a change to the normal course of human events; they're found in God's ability and desire to sustain and nurture people through even the worst situations. Somewhere along the way, I stopped demanding that God fix the problems in my life and started to be thankful for his presence as I endured them." (*Lisa Beamer: Let's Roll: Ordinary People, Extraordinary Courage. Tyndale House Pub; ISBN: 0842373195; (August 20, 2002). "Wrestling with the Whys," pg. 69.*)

Prayer: Great lover, Great forgiver we come as a people who need to learn to be ready, who need to recognize that eternity is only seconds away – according to Your time. Help us recognize we do not live in an "I'll do it tomorrow" society, because we do not know the day or hour that we will face the Heavenly Father's judgment seat. Help each of us "Gain Christ" and be prepared for our final journey. In the name of the Father, Son, and Holy Spirit I pray. Amen.

When We Run Into Problems

"**Oct. 3:** The anti-Taliban Northern Alliance in Afghanistan says it is coordinating an offensive with the U.S. and expects to receive fresh supplies of weapons soon from Iran and Russia. U.S. administration officials say some of the terrorists involved in the attacks also took part in the attack on the USS Cole in Yemen a year ago and the 1998 U.S. Embassy bombings in Africa." *September11News.com*

"There's more to come: We continue to shout our praise even when we're hemmed in with troubles, because we know how troubles can develop passionate patience in us and how that patience in turn forges the tempered steel of virtue, keeping us alert for whatever God will do next. In alert expectancy such as this, we're never left feeling shortchanged. Quite the contrary—we can't round up enough containers to hold everything God generously pours into our lives through the Holy Spirit!" *Romans 5:3-5 (Message Paraphrase)*

Life presents its problems, and you and I are often a part of it. For three service members, it would be the most memorable part of their tour at 9/11 and it only cost them their shirts.

Life was going along as usual, as the mother of four was prepared to travel the subway. She was the in middle of Grand Central Subway Station when it happened. She stopped short in her tracks, as her water broke and she started the delivery of her fifth child in front of a store within Grand Central. It was a rapid delivery overshadowed by God's provision since one of the three soldiers, on duty that day, was a certified EMT. They worked together knowing what to do when they ran into a problem. The baby had a successful arrival, parents were united and soldiers were praised as they provide covering and comfort, for the baby, with their shirts.

I am sure this family and those service members will have a story for their children and grandchildren to remember. The atmosphere of joy remained in the air for a prolonged period that evening, for in the midst of uncertainty and confusion, a new life entered the world. (If I remember correctly, the baby received its name, by parents' request, from all three responders. I am not 100% percent sure, as I received the story and events second-hand from other service members while making my rounds at guard points in and around Grand Central.)

What do we do when we run into a problem? During a time like 9/11, we found we could not always go home to the folks. There were those who wanted to, and I even recommended to those in command that a couple of service members be excused from their obligation.

Our best friend might not be available for comfort and guidance. The First Sergeant tells us he is our best friend, mother and father and whoever we need. He listens to the problem and then tells you:

1. This is how it is done!
2. Find a way and take care of it!
3. Get Over it!

Or, one of my personal favorites is:

4. Go tell it to the Chaplain.

5. He might even tell you to talk to the Commander about it, and the Commander will refer it back to the First Sergeant, and the process starts all over again.

When I run into a problem I personally don't know how to handle, I will often sing, because the words of the songs tell me how others have dealt with their problems, and they help my heart to rejoice even in the midst of my problems.

- *When Upon Life's Billows Roll*

- *Holy, Holy, Holy* is the Lord God Almighty

- *Every Day With Jesus* brings an Eternal Glow

- *Nearer My God to Thee* remains the Lord Almighty

Prayer: Lord, I will admit that many times we come to you because the problems seem so great and we feel so small. Remind us that each trial helps us develop endurance just like each mile that the service member has hiked, run, climbed during their years of military service. Lord, help us find our hope in the Lord along with renewed strength enabling us to rise above each situation and walk through our dark valleys without the strong urge to give up. Thank You Lord. Amen

F.A.M.I.L.Y. United

"**Oct. 4**: NATO allies grant United States access to airfields and seaports, agree to deploy ships and radar planes in war on terrorism." *September11News.com*

"**Oct. 5:** The U.S. Army dispatches 1,000 soldiers to former Soviet republic of Uzbekistan, which borders Afghanistan. Colin Powell extends sanctions on bin Laden's al-Qaida group and 24 other foreign organizations considered terrorist. Armed National Guard patrols begin work at dozens of U.S. airports." *September11News.com*

"But if serving the LORD seems undesirable to you, then choose for yourselves this day whom you will serve, whether the gods your ancestors served beyond the Euphrates, or the gods of the Amorites, in whose land you are living. But as for me and my household, we will serve the LORD." *Joshua 24:15 (NIV)*

The nations were uniting as a family to develop efforts against terrorism. The military was working as a family of multi-branches within the U.S. to establish security. Traditional families were reuniting to strengthen their homes during this cleanup effort.

I met many family units during my time at 9/11 who expressed hardships within their family due to being in New York City serving on guard duty. They shared occasional stories of their family being drawn closer together to support each other and the community they lived in. The pressure of separation and many nights of uncertainty about what tomorrow might bring stressed some relationships but strengthened their resolve to work for relational improvement.

One family in particular suffered a loss of perspective but grew into a family of strength. The daughter who was serving in the National Guard on security detail suffered an emotional breakdown, and we ended up taking her to the hospital. It was wonderful to see her family come together to support her as she headed down her long road toward recovery. She had initially accepted the loss of the Twin Towers and her position to help secure the area. However, she started looking within herself to find her strength and found herself lacking. Therefore, she tried to run from herself as she searched to find herself.

My time ended within the city, and I have no idea if she ever found what she needed. My prayer for her and her family was and is that she found the "Peace of God which passes all understanding" and was able to recognize that she was and never is all alone *(Philippians 4:7)*.

Therefore, at this point in our devotionals I felt a need to present a word that looked at a Biblical guide for the family:

First choice is: me and my family. *(Joshua said in Joshua 24:15)*

A real must is: choosing correctly - "choose this day whom you will serve." *(Joshua 24:15)*

Mighty voice is: knowing the whole truth - He is Lord and He loves you. *(John 3:16)*

Independent life is: learning to walk with God - "...though I walk through the valley..," - you never walk alone. *(Psalm 23:4)(NIV)*

Loving family is: recognizing - "He who finds a wife finds what is good and receives favor from the LORD." *(Proverbs 18:22)* (NIV)

Youthful joy is: living a life that is able to "...rejoice with joy inexpressible and full of glory..." *(1 Peter 1:8 NKJV)*

Scriptures give us many examples of families working together to further the work of God. One such family was: "He (the Centurion) and all his family were devout and God-fearing; he gave generously to those in need and prayed to God regularly." – *Act 10:2*

Prayer: Gracious Father, it is wonderful to know how important family is to You. Help us to develop within our hearts a similar attitude toward our families that we live with, love and serve with, that we might be available to lift up, listen to, and love unconditionally. Give us Godly wisdom and patience that we may complete the journey with victory in our souls and a stronger commitment in our relationships. Amen.

F.R.I.E.N.D.S. Abound

"**Oct. 8:** The FBI takes over the investigation into the Florida anthrax death after the germ was found in the nose of a co-worker and on a computer keyboard in their office. American air strikes on Taliban positions continue for the second day." *September11News.com*

"Oh, how I miss those golden years when God's friendship graced my home,..." *Job 29:1*

Time progresses allowing other area events to overshadow the events of 9/11, as people's lives started to return to what would, for them, be considered normal, realizing in the midst of all their struggles, friends abound.

However, as I looked over the people within the city and listened to those who had the need to express themselves, there were many who still questioned where God was in all this. Many newspaper articles, reporters, and evangelists still asked similar questions. Amidst all the questioning, the friendship of others showed constant strength.

In the Old Testament, Job looked at his life at a time when his friends had abandoned him, a very difficult time of suffering and loss. However, he continued to recognize that God was still around. God was still observing, listening, guarding and caring. He simply was not blessing Job or his family for a reason, but God had not abandoned him – He was still a loving friend.

This truth remains today. He will not abandon you or me either when we face a time of trial or when our friends may seem to offer no support. The Son of God is our best friend who loves us continuously, "a friend who sticks closer than a brother." *(Proverbs 18:24 NIV).* How well do you know this friend of mine? He wants to be your friend as well!

- **F**ind the love of God that is being offered to you.

- **R**each out and touch the Lord as He passes by.

- **I**nspiration is within God's Word written for you

- **E**ncouragement is available for all who cry.

- **N**ever think God has given up or abandoned you

- **D**elightful love is available to cover that heavy sigh.

- **S**elect it, seek it, savor it, and be saved by a Savior who for you did die.

Prayer: Father, sometimes, You seem so far away. I cry and You do not seem to hear me. Lord, in the midst of this turmoil in my life, I need to learn to slow down, look up and listen for that still small voice, that I might recognize that You are the closest friend I could ever have and You would never leave me. Thank You for Your love, support and friendship. Amen.

A.N.D. S.O.?

"**Oct. 9:** FBI agents wearing biohazard suits swarm over the American Media Inc. building in Boca Raton, Florida. All 300 people who work in the building and anyone who spent more than an hour inside since Aug. 1 were advised to visit health officials. American air strikes on Taliban positions continue for the third straight day." *September11 News.com*

"But let all who take refuge in you be glad; let them ever sing for joy. Spread your protection over them that those who love your name may rejoice in you." *Psalm 5:11 (NIV)*

There are the days I look at the news and want to ask – And So? What is going to happen next and how will it affect me?

One day security arrested a phony newspaper photographer who was there to take pictures in a restricted part of the damaged area within the city. Because his identification was a good forgery, he had to be thoroughly searched since he was a person whose first impression was very deceptive. We did not see the real picture or complete picture of what was truly going on with him.

Now what? Or what is next we ask? We ask, ourselves "will life ever return to normal?" But then on the other hand, has life ever been "normal" in New York City? Many have put their life on hold as they help with the cleanup, provide food for the workers, and provide places to sleep; the list goes on. There are those who do not seem anxious to return to what was considered their normal routines knowing their normality has changed.

You and I must recognize that God is one norm in our lives that never changes. We may change in how we see Him, or relate to Him or serve Him. But God can be a constant in our life.

- **A** place of refuge we have found in You

- **N**o need to be troubled within our heart.

- **D**eliverance is something sincerely true.

- **S**o help all in need begin a new start.

- **O**pen our arms - let comfort be found in You.

Prayer: In Your arms, O God is a place of refuge where I can lay my soul bare and know that I will be accepted and forgiven if needed. We look, Lord, at New York City and know the devastation which had been effected. Direct us to come seeking Your personal provision of a new hope and assurance enabling us to start and build a new life with

Your help, removing the questions of uncertainty and the shadows of fear and memory. Replace these feelings with an assurance of a better tomorrow in Your loving presence. Amen.

M.A.N.Y. Perished

"**Oct. 10:** American forces continue to strike military targets in Afghanistan, but the focus for Americans is quickly turning to the anthrax scare." *September11News.com*

"This is the Day the Lord has made, let us rejoice today and be glad in it!" *Psalm 118:24(NIV)*

Our world seems to have people who simply want to cause pain. Many of us working the grounds at and around the 9/11 terrorist attack still witnessed daily where many quickly perished without a second chance at life, and we offer a sigh of sorrow. We look at the activities of our world and see others who look for new avenues that cause others to perish, and I offered a prayer of guidance.

Sorrow seemed to wear a new patch on the service members uniforms as world realities and duty were colliding. Again, the questions: who are we fighting, where are they, what will they do next? It seemed as soon as people were beginning to heal and deal with the crisis, they were called to combat a new enemy. Those serving were beginning to feel a little like Charlie Brown:

"Life is just too much for me," complained Charlie Brown. "I've been confused from the day I was born. I think the whole trouble is that we're thrown into life too fast... we're not really prepared."

"What did you want, a chance to warm up first," asks Linus. – *Charles Schultz – Peanuts*

May the Lord's blessings be – oh – so many!

And may His love for you overflow.

Notice no one is left out – not any.

You have reasons for an inner glow.

"If you know these things, blessed are you if you do them." *John 13:17(NKJV)*

Today, as I look back I still recognize that MANY were affected.

- **M**ay this day be the first of many - more valuable than any treasured penny?

- **A**djusting our attitude every glorious day – celebrating along the way.

- **N**oticing the glory of God all around – listening and enjoying every sound.

- **Y**ielding and giving God all as we strive – this is the day – let us enjoy God's direction and learn to survive.

Prayer: God, let the past be a reminder of the loss we suffered and the losses around the world that have occurred since that time as a result of terrorists, anthrax, floods, hurricanes, earthquakes, tornados or accidents. Let us remember the losses within our lives and be reminded that "This is the Day the Lord has made, let us rejoice…" Psalm 118:24 True, Lord this is an enormous task but I know it is possible through You. Amen.

Many P.E.R.I.S.H.E.D.

"**Oct. 11:** A third person employed by American Media tests positive for anthrax in Florida, and officials say the probe into the source of the disease is now a criminal investigation. President George W. Bush speaks at a memorial service at the Pentagon. Bush vowed to destroy terror with 'every weapon' in the U.S. arsenal as he marked one month since the Sept. 11 attacks at a Pentagon speech. Air strikes continue for the fifth day." *September11News.com*

"For God so loved the world that he gave his one and only Son, that whoever believes in him shall not perish but have eternal life." *John 3:16 (NIV)*

The greatest needed sacrifice came from God, whereas those who were sacrificed at 9/11 did not have a choice. The son of God did! You do! Your choice is for eternity.

- **P**erish – many have for God and Country

- **E**ncouragement comes from many sides.

- **R**eceive the blessing God provides.

- **I**nspire others as you learn of His bounty.

- **S**hed the burdens you have so long tried to hide.

- **H**ope is here – in God is a strong place to abide.

- **E**xperience love that comes from Gods' Loving Arms.

- **D**etermine not to perish covered in God's Holy Charm.

"*USA Today* had an article on the front page about those who escaped the World Trade Center on September 11. After interviewing over 300 survivors and family members of victims, *USA Today* concluded that in the South tower those who didn't delay but ran for safety immediately are the ones who survived. Those who delayed are the ones who perished. It occurred to me that the spiritual life is much the same principle. Those who delay and put off a commitment to Jesus Christ often wait until it's too late.

USA Today also noted that people lived or died in the towers by groups, influenced to stay or go by the people around them. The same is true in our spirituality, that people are often influenced to seek Christ or to reject Christ by those around them.

If there's ever a time for courage, it's in responding to God's call.

Those who didn't delay and who took a stand are those who survived the attack on the World Trade Center.

Those who don't delay and take a stand spiritually are those who respond to God's calling and are saved. If you've never responded to God's call, why don't you do it now as we remember Jesus' sacrifice! "And it shall be that everyone who calls on the name of the Lord will be saved." *Timothy Peck. Edited by SermonCentral Staff. Citation: USA Today 9/3/02*

Prayer: Today let all who read these words choose to accept the gift without hesitation. The gift that You offer, that was paid for by Your death. Help each of us confess our mistakes and accept Your individual forgiveness, Your eternal love and Your salvation. Help us walk through the shadow and into the light. Amen.

Chapter 5

Grace Was Offered (21-33)

"Lord, how do we as a Christian society cope with this sorrow? Let us daily pray God's Blessing"

"I can see how it might be possible to look down upon the earth and be an atheist, but I cannot conceive how he could look into the heavens and say there is no God." — *Abraham Lincoln*

L.O.R.D. Almighty - He makes me lie down in [fresh, tender] green pastures. *Psalm 23:2a (Amplified)*

"**Oct 12:** U.S. President George W. Bush, at the White House celebrating National Hispanic Heritage Month, speaks about the anthrax scare sweeping the nation. Bush tries to reassure Americans that they are safe. American forces continue bombing strategic Taliban positions in Afghanistan." *September11News.com*

When he had finished washing their feet, he put on his clothes and returned to his place. "Do you understand what I have done for you?" he asked them. "You call me 'Teacher' and 'Lord,' and rightly so, for that is what I am. Now that I, your Lord and teacher, have washed your feet, you also should wash one another's feet. *John 13:12-14 (NIV)*

- **L**over: of my life

- **O**wner: of my existence

- **R**edeemer: of my soul

- **D**eliverer: of my sins

"Don't you fear God?" It's a question that I don't think we hear much anymore. And if we're not careful, the next generation will miss entirely this all-important characteristic of God. Disney and Walden Media is releasing C.S. Lewis' *"The Lion, Witch and The Wardrobe"*. In this story, Lewis chose a Lion to represent Jesus. At times the children in the story felt comfortable to run their fingers through his mane, take rides on his back and enjoy being in his presence. But his roar was ferocious enough to introduce an element of fear. It prompted one of the children to ask, "Is Aslan safe?" The thoughtful answer was, "No, He's not safe, but He is good." – *Unknown (Sermoncentral.com/ill)*

My granddaughter, Kerina, Czysz told me one day: "God is good with the Zero (or the nothing) taken out of it." I do not know if this is from her originally or a quote from someone else, but it does summarize this thought well. Many during this time of crisis turned to the Lord and Prayed. It did not matter if they had not talked before to Him. They were ready now because they had heard, seen or experienced the thought and idea that God was and is good.

Prayer: Heavenly Father, Lord Almighty, I come today asking you to help all who serve their country and their community to realize how much You love each and every one of us. God, let us rejoice in the knowledge that You own our lives and that You are Redeemer of our souls and You are truly a good God. Therefore, help us celebrate our deliverance as we continue to pray for those still searching, that they might find the good which you offer to all. In Your name I pray. Amen.

H.O.W. D.O. You Do It?

"**Oct 15:** Suspicious letters and powder are reported at Microsoft offices in Reno, Nevada, and in several countries including Canada, Australia, France, and Germany." *September11News.com*

A service member during the events of 9/11, who knew I was approaching 40 years' service time, asked me, "Why do you continue to serve? You can retire. Haven't you seen enough death and destruction?" My answer is, "yes, I have. However, God has not released me from my call to serve Him in this capacity, therefore I continue as a soldier for Christ."

However, I paused to reflect and when I got a few minutes to myself, I looked up to the heavens and asked, "Lord, how do You do it? How do You continue to love me or others on this earth? How do You continue to forgive us for our despicable acts? How do You continue to freely offer Your best to us who are so unworthy?" God gently reminded me what His Word has shown me over the years:

- **H**ope for tomorrow? – "In *Your* name the nations will put their hope." *(Matthew 12:21 NIV)*

- **O**penness of Your love, when the world wants to hate You? – "Love that never fails." *(1 Corinthians 13:8 NIV)*

- **W**isdom that is for all? – "If any of you lacks wisdom, you should ask God, who gives generously to all without finding fault, and it will be given to you." *(James 1:5 NIV)*

- **D**elight in you and me? – "They confronted me in the day of my disaster, but the LORD was my support. He brought me out into a spacious place; he rescued me because he delighted in me." *(Psalm 18:18-19 NIV)*

- **O**bligation of Yourself toward my life – "I am come that you might have life and have it more abundantly" *(John 10:10 NIV)*

Prayer: Lord, I pray to You this day, knowing it does not make any sense in my mind why You do what You do for the likes of me. I ask you now to "Show me your ways, O LORD, teach me your paths;

guide me in your truth and teach me, for you are God my Savior, and my hope is in you all day long." *Psalm 25:4-5 (NIV).* Amen.

Imposter - W.E. A.S. A. Humble People

"**Oct. 16:** A 7-month-old son of an ABC producer tests positive for anthrax exposure after visiting the building three weeks prior. Microsoft's Bill Gates said the software giant was boosting security measures after six employees were exposed to a letter that tested positive for anthrax. The U.S. military, which first dropped bombs, then food, on Afghanistan, launches a paper propaganda assault. American forces strike Taliban positions for the 9th straight day." *September11News.com*

"If my people, who are called by my name, will humble themselves and pray and seek my face and turn from their wicked ways, then I will hear from heaven, and I will forgive their sin and will heal their land." *2 Chronicles 7:14*

Another exhausting day in the city, and it was reported that there was another imposter, one I would never even consider being so. But there he was, big as life. He was arrested in Grand Central Station. The man was real gutsy or mad, I do not know which! Soldier's spotted him by his mannerisms, not his appearance. He knew how to look the part but not how to live it. He was posing as a Major General (2 star General).

Paul Fritz writes: "Dieter Zander, the pastor of the first GenX church in America, spoke at a conference about reaching people in the age of relativism. He cited a Barna study that asked people to use single words to describe Jesus. They responded: "wise, accepting, compassionate, gracious, humble." Then he asked them to use single words to describe Christians; they said: "critical, exclusive, self-righteous, narrow and repressive."

I ask, with a reminder note to myself, where are you in this evaluation? Are you:

- **W**alking with the Lord as a wonderful event

- **E**ach day walking and feasting in Your truth.

- Acting with new vigor from the Holy Love You sent

- Serving with honor, as we pass through Your examination booth

- **A** = my desired final grade, after passing the test you sent.

"There is a difference between knowing the good news and being the good news," Zander said. "We are the evidence! How we live our lives is the evidence. Everything counts – all the time."

Prayer: Therefore, Lord I pray that You "examine me, GOD, from head to foot, order your battery of tests. Make sure I'm fit inside and out so I never lose sight of your love, but keep in step with you, never missing a beat." For this privilege, I thank you, Lord. Amen. (*Psalm 26:2-3)* (MSG)

The C.H.R.I.S.T.I.A.N. Life

"**Oct. 17:** Palestinian gunmen assassinate far-right Israeli cabinet minister Rehavam Zeevi in revenge for the killing of a militant leader, throwing U.S.-led peace efforts into turmoil. The radical Palestinian Popular Front for the Liberation of Palestine (PFLP) claimed responsibility for shooting Zeevi, a 75-year-old former general who advocated the 'transfer' of Arabs from land claimed by Jews. Israeli Prime Minister Ariel Sharon said the killing marked a major change in Israeli-Palestinian relations. 'The situation is different today, and will not again be like it was yesterday,' he said.

Thirty-one staffers at Tom Daschle's office test positive for anthrax. New York Governor George Pataki speaks to the media at a news conference in New York, and says his offices showed the presence of anthrax in a test and has been closed for further testing and decontamination work." *September11News.com*

"For God did not send his Son into the world to condemn the world, but to save the world through him. Whoever believes in him is not condemned, but whoever does not believe stands condemned already because they have not believed in the name of God's one and only Son." *John 3:17-18*

Howard Hendricks said, "In the midst of a generation screaming for answers, Christians are stuttering."

It was true. It was evident. In New York City at the time of 9/11, there were so many wonderful examples of Christ-like attitude throughout the city, many which I have mentioned already. Two stood out as I visited those on security and clean up during the evening shift.

The first example that stood out was at the Presbyterian Church which sat right outside Ground Zero. The church was open 24 hours a day, with people serving hot soup and sandwiches along with other snacks that hit the right spot at the right time. They also provided a pew to sleep in, with an occasional bed available on the second floor balcony, where I took a few short naps in the middle of the night before heading back to my day-time duties in the command area.

The second example that stood out was at a wonderful restaurant that remained open after normal hours to serve a buffet that would satisfy any hard-working individual. Many of the workers from Ground Zero came along with security personnel to eat there at the early hours of the morning. The food was offered free to all those working within the 9/ll disaster area. Professionalism was seen everywhere in attitude and actions. Christian acts of kindness without the name of Christian on them.

These are some of examples that define what it means to exemplify a Christian life. To put it simply: It is a combination of receiving and giving of available resources mixed with a combination of giving and receiving a personal attitude and desire to love your neighbor.

The Christian Life:

Chooses: to walk in the Light – "… Jesus spoke …, "I am the light of the world. Whoever follows me will never walk in darkness, but will have the light of life.". (John 8:12) (NIV) - and celebrate life.

Hopes: in God's Purpose – "My hope is secure…" individually offered. (Song)

Receives: "What I pass on to you." Let this love carry on to others. (1 Corinthians 15:3) (NIV)

Inspires: "Let us encourage one another" - all sisters and brothers. (1 Thessalonians 5:11) (NIV)

Stands: "On Christ the solid rock I stand…" Helping each to live a life for You. (song)

Tests: "Tribulation works patience…" Lord, I sometimes personally find that hard to do.

Inherits: The Kingdom of God … a present and future projection.

Authorizes: "Greater things shall I do." A powerful expectation

Notices: "A New Creation" – an ongoing and developing relation.

"Evangelism is not what we tell people, unless what we tell is totally consistent with whom we are. It is who we are that is going to make the difference. If we do not truly enjoy our faith, nobody is going to catch the fire of enjoyment from us. If our lives are not totally centered on Christ, we will not be Christ-bearers for others, no matter how pious our words." [Show and Tell, Citation: Madeleine L'Engle, quoted in *Christian Reader* (May/June 1998, p. 50)]

Prayer: Lord, today I ask your help that we might desire to live according to Your Word and "…not conform any longer to the pattern of this world, but be transformed by the renewing of your mind. Then you will be able to test and approve what God's will is—his good, pleasing and perfect will." *Romans 12:2* (NIV) Amen.

Christian S.O.C.I.E.T.Y.

"**Oct. 18:** Two new cases of the skin form of anthrax are reported - one involving an assistant to CBS anchorman Dan Rather and the other a postal worker in New Jersey. That brings to six the total number of confirmed cases of anthrax infection.

…Victory in Afghanistan will require putting troops on the ground in addition to bombing terrorist and Taliban targets from the air, Defense Secretary Donald H. Rumsfeld said at a Pentagon press conference." *September11News.com*

Jesus answered, "It is written in the Scriptures: 'You must worship the Lord your God and serve only him.'" *Luke 4:8 NKJV*

Many say those who serve within the military do not live within or could ever be considered a "Christian Society." Therefore, I would have to ask what describes a Christian Society. Christ can live in any society where He is invited! Regardless of our society, the difficulties of life continue as we fight different forms of enemies. Our efforts to build a Christ like society are represented by our own deeds, actions and attitudes. All apply no matter where we live or serve – civilian or military life.

"Jesus . . . wants us to see that the neighbor next door or the people sitting next to us on a plane or in a classroom are not interruptions to our schedule. They are there by divine appointment. Jesus wants us to see their needs, their loneliness, their longings, and he wants to give us the courage to reach out to them". *Rebecca Manley Pippert*

Our Christian society is moving beyond the norms of human society; we are learning how to serve the Lord, not through mere words, but through actions, personal involvement, and even attitude.

- **S**erving the Lord is:

- **O**pening to His love,

- **C**hoosing His pleasure

- **I**dentifying His purpose

- **E**xtending His outreach

- **T**outing His wisdom

- **Y**ielding to His authority

Prayer: Lord, help us to worship You first. Then help us be willing to share our worship, our joy, our peace, our comfort, and our understanding, as we reach out to all our neighbors, the seen and the currently unseen. Lord, the city still contains too many unseen people. Help those who live there see with new eyes and expand their society with words of hope and encouragement, which can be found only in God. In Your name we pray. Amen.

Lord Help Me C.O.P.E.

"**Oct. 19:** U.S. ground forces battle in Afghanistan, opening a new phase of the war on terrorism after nearly two weeks of fierce air strikes, a defense official said. The anthrax strains surfacing with terrifying impact in Florida, New York and Washington are all similar, said Bush officials, likely indicating a single source. 'We obviously are preparing for more,' said homeland security chief Tom Ridge. A second New Jersey mail carrier is confirmed to have skin anthrax." *September11News.com*

- So Jesus said to those Jews [This applies to you and me also] who believe in Him, "If you abide in My word [hold fast to My teachings and live in accordance with them], you are truly My disciples." *(John 18:31 Amplified)*
- "… you will know the Truth, and the Truth will set you free." *(John 18:31 Amplified)*

More than a month has passed, and I still see too many walking around with self-imposed chains, warring within themselves because they had lived while others had died. Their stories, when they look back, seem insignificant, but they changed their destinies:

1. The head of a company who survived 9/11 because his son started kindergarten that day, and the dad took him to school.
2. Another man was alive because 9/11 was his day to get the donuts.
3. One could not get a taxi to get to work on time.

The truth for life, for peace, for comfort, for strength is found within the Holy Book we call the Bible. In these words, we will always be reminded that God has a plan for you and me. We are here for a reason.

Therefore I say, Lord help us:

- **C**hoose to obey Your glorious Holy Word,

- **O**pen our hearts to receive Your Unconditional Love,

- **P**resent Your Truths to everyone about their Lord

- **E**xperience new victories with help from above.

"Shake it off and step up," perfectly illustrates the concept of dealing with disappointment. "A parable is told of a farmer who owned an old mule. The mule fell into the farmer's well. The farmer heard the mule braying. After carefully assessing the situation, the farmer sympathized with the mule, but decided that neither the mule nor the well was worth the trouble of saving. Instead, he called his neighbors together and told them what had happened...and enlisted them to help haul dirt to bury the old mule in the well and put him out of his misery.

Initially, the old mule was hysterical, but as the farmer and his neighbors continued shoveling and the dirt hit his back...a thought struck him. It suddenly dawned on him that every time a shovel load of dirt landed on his back...*he should shake it off and step up*. This he did, blow after blow. 'Shake it off and step up...shake it off and step up...shake it off and step up' he repeated to encourage himself. No matter how painful the blows, or distressing the situation seemed, the old mule fought panic and just kept right on shaking it off and stepping up.

It wasn't long before the old mule, battered and exhausted, stepped triumphantly over the wall of the well. What seemed as something which would bury him actually blessed him…all because of the manner in which he handled his adversity." Author unknown – SermonCentral .com

Disappointment can make or break us, depending on how we cope with it. The shadows of disappointment can linger or we can walk through it.

Prayer: Lord, sometimes my daily life seems hard to cope with, and then a problem adds to it, and I forget to turn to You for help. Allow those with the words of encouragement to enter my life, and let Your Son be the source of needed forgiveness, healing and spiritual growth that enables me to grow. Help me, Lord, to learn to shake it off and step up to any challenge You bring my way. Lord, let my strength to cope come from You that I may truly rejoice in Your provisions. Amen.

W.I.T.H. T.H.I.S. I Dwell in Safety

"**Oct. 20:** Elite U.S. Rangers launch raids into Afghanistan in the dark of night. Two U.S. soldiers are killed when their helicopter crashes in Pakistan near the Afghanistan border. In China, Bush says the soldiers 'did not die in vain.' … Paul McCartney and dozens of stars perform at a benefit concert in New York City.

Oct 21: The 21 - member APEC countries, meeting in Shanghai China, end their conference and issue a joint statement denouncing terrorism. … two postal workers at the Brentwood postal facility in Washington D.C. are confirmed with anthrax and are hospitalized. Tests begin on hundreds of Washington postal workers.

 Oct 22: U.S. Defense Secretary Rumsfeld scolds the press for troop movement leaks that may jeopardize lives or missions. Air strikes in Afghanistan continue with a focus on Taliban troops in Northern Afghanistan. Two Washington postal workers die mysteriously. Anthrax is the suspected cause." *September11News.com*

"I will lie down and sleep in peace, for you alone, O LORD, make me dwell in safety." *Psalm 4:8 (NIV 1984)*

Safety was a word we were very conscious of as we lived and worked in New York City after the terrorist attacks: safety as rescuers and their dogs searched the rubble, safety as steel beams were hoisted, loaded and hauled away. Safety was a key element for protection and security, while personnel worked in harm's way.

There is an ongoing safety that comes from meeting and growing in the love of God. I am reminded of this in the cute story by an unknown author about a little old lady:

A little old lady was amazed at how nice the young man was next door. Every day he would help her gather things from her car or help her in her yard. One day, the old lady finally asked the young man, "Son, how did you become such a fine young man?"

The young man replied, "Well, when I was a boy, I had a drug problem."

The old lady was shocked. "I can't believe that."

The young man replied, "It's true. My parents drug me to church on Sunday morning, drug me to church on Sunday night and drug me to church on Wednesday night."

With reflection like that we can say:

- **W**onderful days before us I now see

- **I** come now into Your presence to be.

- **T**he day shines brightly filled with Your glory

- **H**umbly, I desire to be part of Your love story.

With Your Love in our lives we can **T**aking **H**ome **I**ndividual **S**erenity.

In all my time within the city, I felt quite secure. I was sometimes lost by the enormousness of the area and the number of people, but I felt safe. Of course traveling under God's guidance I believe has always been a strong asset.

Isn't it wonderful that you and I are offered something so wonderful; peace, safety and security? It is our choice, our opportunity, our possibility, and one of the rewards sent from God to each and every individual who chooses to accept His love.

Prayer: Lord, in our life You are able to bring a strong endearing sense of serenity. Help each of us find the peace that leads to a life of contentment. There are so many of us who are troubled, hurting, and needing as we serve both our God and our country. Lead us to a place of inner peace we pray. Amen.

Overcome S.O.R.R.O.W.

"**Oct. 23:** Two postal workers from the Brentwood postal facility in Washington are confirmed to have died from inhalation anthrax. Another New Jersey postal worker is confirmed with anthrax. Anthrax is confirmed in a Washington facility that sorts White House mail. The FBI releases photographs of the letters, confirmed to carry anthrax spores, that were sent to Tom Daschle, Tom Brokaw, and the Editor of the NY Post. The IRA promises to disarm 'to save the peace process' in Northern Ireland." *September11News.com*

"My soul is weary with sorrow; strengthen me according to your word." *Psalm 119:28 (NIV)*

Sorrow comes in many packages and can be seen daily in the news media. Some sorrow runs deep, and people do not know how to escape. I found my sorrow triggered many times when I passed a wall of photos of those who were missing and those who were found and now personally missed.

It was in the early part of the winter months, and temperatures were below freezing. A young soldier was sitting quietly gazing at the surrounding area outside his two-person guard shack. I sat with him as we exchanged the pleasantries of the day. After a short period of time to deepen the conversation, I asked him if he was looking forward to finishing his tour, so he could return home and get back to work. The silence was eerie as he paused hesitating; looked about, and then responded, saying he did not have a job to go home to. He worked within one of the towers, and his company was no longer there. I sat silently with him for a short time, offered my condolences and asked if he desired prayer. I had no answers for him. I could only offer comfort and support. We prayed and I moved on with a personal sense of loss.

Obviously grief and sorrow have been a powerful part of our country and individual lives since 9/11.

Prayer: Lord we are grateful that you comfort us during our times of sorrow. We see comfort and direction in your Word.

- **"S**earch me, O Lord, ... and see if there is any wicked way in me." (Psalm 139:23-24 NKJV)

- **O**pen my eyes clarifying the audacious truth You have for me.

- **R**evive my soul with a renewing of your Holy Spirit alive in me.

- **R**elieve my guilt for my mistakes of the day, that Your Genuine Love I might see.

- **O**pen my arms to those around who need a personal blessing through me,

- **W**illing to serve – help me to be the person You desire me to be. Amen.

Come L.E.T. U.S.

"**Oct. 24:** Israel continues to raid Palestinian controlled areas, and claims to have captured two of the Zeevi assassins. U.S. Postmaster General John Potter tells Americans 'There are no guarantees that mail is safe.' He also advises Americans to wash hands after handling mail. An air strike in Kabul kills 22 Pakistani militants linked to Osama bin Laden. The U.S. House of Representatives overwhelmingly approves a domestic anti-terrorism bill giving police new powers. Pentagon says they are 'surprised at how doggedly' the Taliban are clinging to power." *September11News.com*

"Let us examine our ways and test them, and let us return to the LORD. Let us lift up our hearts and our hands to God in heaven, …." *Lamentations 3:40 – 41 (NIV)*

The Lord through His Word warns us about the pitfalls of life and gives us support and guidance. His desire is that you and I live with inner peace. History shows us turmoil. Those within New York City at this time were doing their best to reestablish a form of peace.

Peace is something I personally have experienced, many times through God's inner presence, since the days of Viet Nam. God offers peace, in the midst of a world continually filled with ongoing, seemingly unending, struggles.

Let us: two simple words that are repeated numerous times, that provide answers, that touch a multitude of lives and opens doors in the healing process.

How many times have you joined the crowd and said **Let Us**? Did you mean it? Were you willing to join the Lord and work together by serving Him? "Let us therefore make every effort to do what leads to peace and to mutual edification." – *Romans 14:19. (NIV)*

"So **let us come** to him with a true heart. **Let us come** because we believe all these things. **Let us come** with our hearts washed clean from our wrong ways. **Let us come** with our bodies washed with clean water. We must hold on to God's promise that we have said we believed. And we must never let go. He has promised and he will do it. **Let us think** of one another and help one another to love and to do good things." – *Hebrews 10:22-25 (*WE)

Today in order to strive toward our own inner peace notice how God's Word **warns** us toward life in Him:

Worship: "**Let us** go to his dwelling place; **let us worship** at his footstool…" – *Psalm 132:7 (NIV)*

Acknowledge: "**Let us acknowledge** the LORD; **let us press on** to acknowledge him. As surely as the sun rises, he will appear; he will come to us like the winter rains, like the spring rains that water the earth." – *Hosea 6:3 (NIV 84)*

Rejoice: "The LORD has done it this very day; **let us rejoice** today and be glad.". – *Psalm 118:24 (NIV)*

Not: **"Let us not become weary** in doing good, for at the proper time we will reap a harvest if we do not give up. Therefore, as we have opportunity, **let us** do good to all people, especially to those who belong to the family of believers." – *Galatians 6:9 – 10* (NIV)

Stop: "Therefore **let us stop passing judgment** on one another. Instead, make up your mind not to put any stumbling block or obstacle in your brother's way." – *Romans 14:13 (NIV)*

Prayer: Lord, as we look at the many Scriptures, "only **Let Us Live** up to what we have already attained." *(Philippians 3:16) (NIV).* **Let Us Pray** with sincerity and appreciation for Your Powerful Words and Mighty Love in order to honor You. "Dear children, **Let Us NOT** love with words or tongue but with actions and in truth." *(1 John 3:18)* (NIV) Amen.

D.A.I.L.Y. Serve

"**Oct. 25:** Under extreme pressure from the U.S. and other countries, Israel agrees to begin withdrawal from occupied Palestinian territory. U.S. Vice President Dick Cheney said homeland security is not temporary, and 'will become permanent in American life.'…. Anthrax at Capitol Hill is described as very high quality." *September11News .com*

"…when you pray, go into your room, close the door and pray to your Father, who is unseen. Then your Father, who sees what is done in secret, will reward you. *Matthew 6:6 (NIV)*

There were certain guard positions I looked forward to visiting more than others. They were favorites, because I knew at the end of my visit, the service member would ask that we join in prayer. Sometimes, with selfish motives, I needed the prayer for my own strength and continued ministry.

Jeff Strite stated: "Always pray and don't give up."

"Jesus taught that we should 'always pray and not give up.'
- "Not because God is hard of hearing
- Not because God needs to be pestered into answering our requests
- Not because God doesn't want to answer us
- Not because God has call waiting and will get back to us.

"No. Jesus taught us always pray and not give up, because when we pray, our prayers carry weight. Every time you and I pray, we unleash more and more power from the throne of God.

Are you praying for someone in your family to become a Christian? Every prayer you pray puts more and more pressure on that person to listen to God.

Do you pray for your friends in their daily struggles? Every prayer you pray imparts to them more and more power from God.

Do you have difficulties with someone at work? Every prayer you lift up to God's throne brings God's power to bear on difficult people and situations.

Prayer is not a passive act on our part. Prayer is AN AGGRESSIVE, ACTIVE MINISTRY. You are putting your shoulder to the wheel and moving the forces of heaven." *Jeff Strite in "The Power of Persistent Prayer"*

Members of the military learn very quickly the importance of a daily existence, a daily preparation, a daily outlook, because you have no idea where you will be or what you may be doing the next day. You live for the day by preparing for the uncertainties of tomorrow. I found it not unusual to discover that a guard point had moved between the times of visiting early morning shift personal and completing my evening rounds. The personal frustration came when I was not informed.

Today, as we trudge through the shadow of death, we join the litany when we pray familiar verses: 'Give us this day our **DAILY** bread' *(Matthew 6:11)*, or we are encouraged to "take up *our* cross **DAILY** and follow *You*" *(Luke 9:23)*. We are instructed "that *our* **DAILY** life may win the respect of outsiders" *(1 Thessalonians 4:12)* and to "...encourage one another **DAILY**, as long as it is called 'Today,' so that none of you may be hardened by sin's deceitfulness." *(Hebrews 3:13)*.

Our walk with God is to be a **DAILY** one.

- **D**o You Really Want The Best,

- **A**llow God To Be Part Of Your Life.

- **I**nspire Others Along This Quest.

- **L**ive In Victory Amidst The Strife,

- **Y**ou Can Ask God To Give You Rest

Prayer: Lord help us **DAILY** to "Come unto You, all of us that labor and are heavy laden,(knowing) ... You will give us rest." *(Matthew 11:28 NKJV)*. Your Word shows us so many promises which are affirmed through our prayer conversation with You and Your Son. Lord, will You infiltrate us with these promises that they may flow through our lives to influence others, that they too may find Your comforting presence in the reminders of death. Amen.

Daily P.R.A.Y.

"**Oct. 26:** U.S. President George W. Bush signs the anti-terrorism bill into law. Britain announces that 200 elite commandos were ready for action in the U.S.-led coalition. A small amount of anthrax spores are found in a CIA mailroom." *September11News.com*

"When you pray, don't babble on and on as people of other religions do. They think their prayers are answered merely by repeating their words again and again. Don't be like them, for your Father knows exactly what you need even before you ask Him! Pray like this: Our Father in heaven, may Your name be kept holy. *(Matthew 6:7-9) NLT*

There were a few, as I mentioned before, who looked forward to my coming because of their strong desire to join in prayer. Many others were willing to discuss problems and concerns, recognizing that God could help. Often they did not want to pray about it. I found that disheartening, because I believe God does answer prayers. He does want us to ask, expecting results.

Moments of answered prayers were seen, but many answers never seemed to come about. I believe this happens because specific request were never asked. I'll be honest: I have my times when faith is weak, but I have learned from experience that God answers prayers in three ways: Yes, No and Wait a while. But He does answer prayers.

From an article entitled, "<u>What My Mother Taught Me</u>," (Author Unknown) I liked the following statement: "My mother taught me religion: When I spilled grape juice on the carpet, she instructed, 'You better pray the stain will come out of the carpet."

- **P**ut your thoughts in His hands

- **R**ecognize God's commands

- **A**llow Him to guide within your lands

- **Y**ield yourself to His demands

Helen Roseveare, a medical missionary and author from England wrote an article entitled:

A Little Girl's Prayer

One night I had worked hard to help a mother in the labor ward; but in spite of all we could do she died, leaving us with a tiny premature baby and a crying two-year-old daughter. We would have difficulty keeping the baby alive, as we had no incubator (we had no electricity to run an incubator) and no special feeding facilities.

Although we lived on the equator, nights were often chilly with treacherous drafts. One student midwife went for the box we had for such babies and the cotton wool the baby would be wrapped in. Another went to stoke up the fire and fill a hot water bottle. She came back shortly in distress to tell me that in filling the bottle, it had burst. Rubber perishes easily in tropical climates. "And it is our last hot water bottle!" she exclaimed. As in the West it is no good crying over spilled milk, so in Central Africa it might be considered no good crying over burst water bottles. They do not grow on trees, and there are no drugstores down forest pathways.

"All right," I said, "Put the baby as near the fire as you safely can; sleep between the baby and the door to keep it free from drafts. Your job is to keep the baby warm."

The following noon, as I did most days, I went to have prayers with any of the orphanage children who chose to gather with me. I gave the youngsters various suggestions of things to pray about and told them about the tiny baby. I explained our problem about keeping the baby warm enough, mentioning the hot water bottle. The baby could so easily die if it got chills. I also told them of the two-year-old sister, crying because her mother had died.

During the prayer time, one ten-year-old girl, Ruth, prayed with the usual blunt conciseness of our African children. "Please, God," she prayed, "send us a water bottle. It'll be no good tomorrow, God, as the baby will be dead, so please send it this afternoon."

While I gasped inwardly at the audacity of the prayer, she added by way of corollary, "And while You are about it, would You please send a dolly for the little girl so she'll know You really love her?"

As often with children's prayers, I was put on the spot. Could I honestly say, "Amen"? I just did not believe that God could do this. Oh, yes, I know that He can do everything. The Bible says so. But there are limits, aren't there? The only way God could answer this particular prayer would be by sending me a parcel from the homeland. I had been in Africa for almost four years at that time, and I had never, ever, received a parcel from home; anyway, if anyone did send me a parcel, who would put in a hot water bottle? I lived on the equator!

Halfway through the afternoon, while I was teaching in the nurses' training school, a message was sent that there was a car at my front door. By the time I reached home, the car had gone, but there, on the veranda, was a large twenty-two pound parcel. I felt tears pricking my eyes. I could not open the parcel alone, so I sent for the orphanage children. Together we pulled off the string, carefully undoing each knot. We folded the paper, taking care not to tear it unduly. Excitement was mounting. Some thirty or forty pairs of eyes were focused on the large cardboard box.

From the top, I lifted out brightly colored, knitted jerseys; eyes sparkled as I pulled them out. Then there were the knitted bandages for the leprosy patients, and the children looked a little bored. Then came a box of mixed raisins and sultanas --- that would make a nice batch of buns for the weekend. Then, as I put my hand in again, I felt the ..... could it really be? I grasped it and pulled it out --- yes, a brand-new, rubber hot water bottle! I cried. I had not asked God to send it; I had not truly believed that He could.

Ruth was in the front row of the children. She rushed forward, crying out, "If God has sent the bottle, He must have sent the dolly, too!" Rummaging down to the bottom of the box, she pulled out the small, beautifully dressed dolly. Her eyes shone! She had never doubted.

Looking up at me, she asked: "Can I go over with you, Mummy, and give this dolly to that little girl, so she'll know that Jesus really loves her?"

That parcel had been on the way for five whole months. Packed up by my former Sunday school class, whose leader had heard and obeyed God's prompting to send a hot water bottle, even to the equator. And one of the girls had put in a dolly for an African child --- five months before --- in answer to the believing prayer of a ten-year old to bring it "that afternoon." *~By Helen Roseveare*

Prayer: Heavenly Father, I do desire Your Name be honored. I offer You praise this day, asking You to help us as a society, to celebrate the answers You provide. Help us join You with a new heart that desires to talk to and with You. Help us be like the children who ask and actually expect to receive because You know what we need before we ask. Thank you, Lord. Amen.

G.O.D.'S. Blessing

"**Oct. 28:** For the second straight day civilians are killed in heavy U.S. air strikes in Kabul. Gunmen stormed into a Christian church in Behawalpur, Pakistan, during Sunday services, and sprayed the congregation with gunfire, killing the minister and 15 others. Israeli tanks leave Bethlehem after Prime Minister Ariel Sharon gave the green light for withdrawal despite attacks by Palestinians that killed five people in Israel. A New Jersey postal worker is diagnosed with inhalation anthrax. A WTC memorial service, attended by victim's families, is held in New York City at 'Ground Zero,' amidst the still smoldering ruins." *September11News.com*

The memorial service was a day of remembrance, hope and sorrow for many families. The sorrow expressed was pitch black and deep that night. The remembrance was greatly appreciated. However, it being a remembrance it was also an affirmation finalizing the loss of many loved ones.

Sometimes we find within the darkness a glimmer of light, and other times not even a shadow. To the service members this night, there were many shadows of uncertainty once again revealed about life and how God blesses, provides and protects. Some old questions were called to mind, and I found, too often, I did not really know how to respond – except mostly with a word of prayer.

There is a Swedish proverb which says: "Worry often gives a small thing a big shadow." We all have our fears.

Micah, who was considered one of the Minor Prophets in the Old Testament, had an interesting description of what was to come. This was prophetic of what was and still is to happen to each of us as we consider the memories of 9/11. If you believe, as I do – God knows what He is doing even though we do not see His handiwork. God has a plan, and you and I do fit into it if we desire. Man may bring about event that were not an original part of God's Plan but God knows how to put things in perspective.

God's Blessings will remove the fear

"In days to come the mountain where the Temple stands

will be the highest one of all, towering above all the hills.

Many nations will come streaming to it, and their people will say,

"Let us go up the hill of the Lord, to the Temple of Israel's God.

He will teach us what he wants us to do.

We will walk in the paths he has chosen.

For the Lord's teaching comes from Jerusalem;

from Zion he speaks to his people."

He will settle disputes among the nations,

among the great powers near and far.

They will hammer their swords into plows

and their spears into pruning knives.

Nations will never again go to war, never prepare for battle again.

Everyone will live in peace among his own vineyards and fig trees,

and no one will make him afraid.

The Lord Almighty has promised this."

(Micah 4:1-4) (GNT)

Think about this passage – what a promise! It is an Old Testament passage from a prophet who had been appointed to deliver this message. It was a message given for the time, under the rules of God. It is a message for today as we live under the grace of God, which is found in the love of Christ. "The Lord Almighty has promised this."

- **G**od surrounds each gently with love

- **O**bserve His loving presence is here

- **D**etermine to find strength from above

- **S**tand with Him and victoriously cheer

Prayer: Lord God Almighty, today we thank You for Your many promises and everlasting presence. We ask that You will lead us to recognize Your Holy Arms of protection, breath of hope, and Holy Spirit's inner presence and peace, as we strive for "Peace on Earth and Good Will Toward Men," by living our lives moving, beyond the shadows, toward eternal peace. In Your name we pray. Amen.

God's B.L.E.S.S.I.N.G.

"**Oct. 30:** The Federal Aviation Administration imposes flight restrictions around U.S. nuclear plants and advises 103 nuclear facilities to fortify security. Alert warnings issued on Oct. 29 are based on information from Canadian intelligence officials. A Manhattan hospital worker with inhalation anthrax is 'struggling for survival.'" *September11News.com*

"Blessed is the person who does not walk in the counsel of the wicked." *Psalm 1:1 NKJV*

When you read the news, it does not sound like we should be rejoicing much or that we are being blessed. The number of times I have sung in church, "count your blessings, name them one by one," I cannot tell you. But I know that the times I have actually sat down and counted my blessings have been very few.

New orders have arrived and new locations were established. This would be the first day, I made my rounds visiting service members who received their new assignments to the nuclear plants. I witnessed a new sense of fear. A new shadow was seen that, once again awoke not so distant memories. It was fear mixed with uncertainty, based upon rumors and ideas concerning the dangers of their new mission. We talked with a high level of frustration pondering the ideal choice of not being there. We honestly had to admit that if the nuclear plant was hit, there would be literally nothing left of us but a big hole in the ground. These were sobering conversations. It made it difficult for many to even consider counting blessings.

Max Lucado related a terrific story of a man who knew how to count his blessings entitled: **"Everything I Need."**

"I have everything I need for joy!" Robert Reed said.

His hands are twisted and his feet are useless. He can't bathe himself. He can't feed himself. He can't brush his teeth, comb his hair, or put on his underwear. Strips of Velcro hold his shirts together. His speech drags like a worn out audiocassette.

Robert has cerebral palsy.

The disease keeps him from driving a car, riding a bike, and going for a walk. But it didn't keep him from graduating from high school or attending Abilene Christian University, from which he graduated with a degree in Latin. Having cerebral palsy didn't keep him from teaching at St. Louis Junior College or from venturing overseas on five mission trips. And Robert's disease didn't prevent him from becoming a missionary in Portugal.

He moved to Lisbon, alone, in 1972. There he rented a hotel room and began studying Portuguese. He found a restaurant owner who would feed him after the rush hour and a tutor who would instruct him in the language.

Then he stationed himself daily in a park, where he distributed brochures about Christ. Within six years he led seventy people to the Lord, one of whom became his wife, Rosa."

Rev. Max Lucado continued by saying: "I heard Robert speak recently. I watched other men carry him in his wheelchair onto the platform. I watched them lay a Bible in his lap. I watched his stiff fingers force open the pages. And I watched people in the audience wipe away tears of admiration from their faces. Robert could have asked for sympathy or pity, but he did just the opposite. He held his bent hand up in the air and boasted, "I have everything I need for joy."

"His shirts are held together by Velcro, but his life is held together by joy." *(Max Lucado)*

My question for you to consider: What do you define as a blessing?

- **B**ring the day before your Maker

- **L**isten to the World's Greatest Shaker

- **E**xperience One who really cares

- **S**pend time with One who sincerely shares

- **S**ee what He has within His store

- **I**nquire – is there truly much more?

- **N**ever assume – we know what that does

- **G**row and develop – then follow God's Buzz

Prayer: Lord I thank You for the many blessings You have brought into my life and look forward to those still to come. I ask Your additional blessings on those still dealing with the shadow of death that hangs over them from the events of 9/11. Bless all who are battling within this day; each person, family, and situation. Bless those who choose to come and receive from You. Let the reality of Your blessings be genuinely experienced. In Your name I pray. Amen.

Chapter 6

Exception Was Seen (34-42)

*". . .upon Soldiers, Marines, Sailors, Coast Guards and Airmen now
serving"*

> *"Each day – and particularly on this historic day – we honor the
> men and women in uniform who serve our country and protect
> our freedom. They travel to the dangerous corners of the world,
> and we must remember that for every person who is in uniform,
> there are families who wait for them to come home safely."*
> Tiger Woods at an inauguration celebration for President-elect
> Barack Obama.

U.P.O.N. Solid Ground

"**Oct. 31:** The French newspaper *Le Figaro* claims that Osama bin
Laden stayed for 10 days in a Dubai hospital in July, 2001 for treatment
of a serious kidney ailment. Under heavy security, two armored
vehicles transported $200 million in gold from a Bank of Nova Scotia
vault located in the ruins of the World Trade Center. Taliban forces in
northern Afghanistan are hit with heavy bombardment from B-52
bombers, indicating possible preparedness for Northern Alliance troop

movements on Taliban positions. A NY hospital worker dies from inhaled anthrax, becoming the first anthrax death not linked to the postal service or the news media." *September11News.com*

"Trust in the Lord with all your heart: and lean not upon your own understanding" *Proverbs 3:5 NKJV*

Our world sure is a complicated place, and our service members face many situations and different types of people. It becomes extremely difficult to not lean on our own understanding when we face situations that require quick responses. Therefore, as a chaplain, it becomes important to help others, military and civilian, learn that the safest place and most secure foundation is found in God. We do not have to understand; we simply need to trust.

A.B. Simpson writes: "In the upper portion of New York City, many citizens may often have noticed, especially in the past years, a great number of miserable shanties standing on the choicest sites. Here they stood on the corner of a splendid new avenue or looking out on a magnificent prospect. These houses were utterly unworthy of the location. Suppose a millionaire should want to purchase this site and that the owner would begin, before giving possession, to repair the old shanty for the new owner putting fresh thatch on the miserable roof and a new coat of whitewash on the dirty walls.

How the purchaser would laugh at him and say, "My friend, I do not want your miserable old wreck of a tenement fixed up like this. At the best, it will only be a shanty when you have done all you can to it, and I will never live in it. All I want is the ground, the site, and when I get it, I will raze the old heap of rubbish to the foundations and dig deep down to the solid rock before I build my splendid mansion. I will then build from the base my own new house according to my own magnificent plan. I do not want a vestige of your house; all that I require is the location."

This is exactly what God wants of us and waits to do in us. Each of us has a splendid site for a heavenly temple. It looks out upon eternity and commands a view of all that is glorious in the possibilities of existence. The house that is built upon it now, however, is a worthless wreck; it is past improving. Our patching and repairing is worse than waste. What God wants of us is simply that we give him the possibilities of our lives, and let him build upon them a temple of holiness which he will make his own abode and which he will let us dwell in with him as his happy guests in the house of the Lord forever." *(A.B. Simpson, founder of the Christian and Missionary Alliance, in his book Wholly Sanctified.)*

U.P.O.N. The Solid Rock

• Understanding is not our task

- **P**lace trust in God is all He is requiring

- **O**bserve and delight in His presence bask

- **N**ow sit back and do some genuine admiring

Benjamin Franklin's famous words tell us: "Be cheerful – the problems that worry us most are those that never arrive."

I am reminded about those who stood guard duty around Ground Zero. Some had a tent to go into; others remain outside for the duration of their duty. Some had the pleasure of performing their duty in front of a exercise facility, whereas others had a fire barrel to stand beside. There were those who stood at the entrance to the tunnels and others on the major interchanges. All served on solid ground with a purpose, as they were watching for the unusual, the different, with orders to stop and search vehicles if necessary. Their solid footing was there, searching to prevent others from removing the physical foundation from us.

Prayer: Heavenly Father, Great Creator of all things, we come with grateful hearts for a place that is solid and sound to place our feet. Now help us to place our hearts also on a spiritually solid ground that would provide security throughout the remainder of our lives. Amen.

S.O.L.D.I.E.R.S. Serve

"**Nov. 1:** The FBI announces it has alerted law enforcement agencies in eight Western U.S. states that it has unconfirmed information terrorists may be targeting suspension bridges on the West Coast. Pakistani press sources say the Taliban have arrested 25 followers of tribal leader Hamid Karzai, and plan to execute them. American warplanes attack Kabul for the first time in four days, striking targets in the northern edge of the capital. In a letter sent to Al-Jazeera TV, Osama bin Laden urges fellow Muslims to rise up against the "Christian Crusade." The fear of anthrax spreads to the Midwest with a finding of contamination at a Kansas City postal facility." *September11News.com*

"…suffer hardship with me as a Good Soldier of Christ Jesus." *II Timothy 2:3 NASB*

There are many who have chosen to serve in the military, recognizing the possibilities of injury or even death. Today's service members do their duty as voluntary members. However, when I was first invited into the military in 1966, it was an offer I could not refuse. There were many even then, who, once called were willing to pay the ultimate sacrifice if necessary. There were even some who volunteered to serve both God and country as well as show honor to their flag.

- So quickly they answered the call

- **O**penly responding – one and all.

- Lives have been put on uncertain hold

- Duties performed in both heat and cold

- Inspiration to our nation – they are,

- Each one reaching to those near and far.

- Rejoice in their efforts that provide a way,

- Showing how loving support saves the day.

Matthew Rogers writes about attending a military funeral for Vernon "Slim" Paaren:

"The key symbol was the American flag. As it was being folded by the service people, one of the veterans who had fired the three shot gun salute began to speak. He said the flag is a symbol of our freedom. "The red stripes represent the blood of those who gave their lives to protect our freedoms. The white stripes signify the purity and innocence of freedom itself. The blue field with white stars represents the great wide sky that stretches across our land, reminding us that we are truly one nation under God."

Prayer: Today, Lord, we pray for our military, especially the soldier, the ground pounder, many of whom are pulling the guard duty at Ground Zero. Help us, Lord, be individuals who show, express and offer our genuine support. We are not able to do it on our own. Amen.

M.A.R.I.N.E.S. March

"**Nov. 2:** Homeland Defense Secretary Tom Ridge issues an 'indefinite' high alert against an undefined terrorist attack. Hundreds of New York firemen march to Ground Zero in an emotional protest over Mayor Giuliani's decision to scale back the number of workers searching for victims. A U.S. Special Forces helicopter crashes in bad weather in Afghanistan. The injured crew members are rescued by another helicopter on the same mission. The downed chopper is later destroyed by F-14 jets." *September11News.com*

"Where two or three are gathered together in My name, there am I in the midst of them." *Matthew 18:20 (NIV)*

The Marines march and often are the first to take the beachhead. They get things started and prepare the road for others to follow. They are also very human. I met a Marine, whom I have a great deal of respect for because he was willing to admit his fears. He came to me telling of his heroic service to this point in his life. Then 9/11 happened. This was his home town, his home land, where he grew up and his family lived. He could not understand nor accept the loss of his homeland. It weighed heavy on his mind and heart. He, at this point in his life, wanted out of his military obligation. After periods of discussion, I talked to his command and recommended the serviceman be allowed to temporally leave with the option to return upon his readiness. Command agreed.

The Marines often have their own story to tell. One Marine sent this letter home:

Hey Dad, "Do me a favor and label this "The Marine," and send it to everybody on your email list . . . I want this rolling all over the US; I want every home reading it, every eye seeing it, and every heart to feel it."

THE MARINE

By: Corporal Aaron M. Gilbert, US Marine Corps

"We all came together, both young and old

To fight for our freedom; to stand and be bold.

In the midst of all evil, we stand our ground,

And we protect our country, from all terror around.

Peace and not war, Is what some people say.

But I'll give my life, so you can live the American way.

I give you the right, to talk of your peace.

To stand in your groups, and protest in our streets.

But still I fight on, I don't bitch, I don't whine.

I'm just one of the people, who is doing your time.

I'm harder than nails, stronger than any machine.

I'm the immortal soldier, I'm a US. MARINE!

So stand in my shoes, and leave from your home.

Fight for the people who hate you,

With the protests they've shown.

Fight for the stranger, Fight for the young.

So they all may have,

The greatest freedom you've won .

Fight for the sick, fight for the poor

Fight for the cripple, who lives next door.

But when your time comes, do what I've done.

For if you stand up for freedom,

You'll stand when the fight's done.

USS SAIPAN, PERSIAN GULF – March 23, 2003

- **M**arching orders have been received.

- **A**ctions established and goals achieved,

- **R**easons may not be fully understood.

- **I**ndividuals who do as they should,

- **N**eeding Godly guidance along the way.

- **E**ach gladly willing to serve this day,

- **S**upport them – daily – unite and pray.

Prayer: Lord, we are not always ready to serve; therefore, we ask for your strength to receive our marching orders. Let us see our individual goals from you and do our part to serve willingly supporting one another in the love of Christ. Lord, if you charge us to take the beachhead first; guide us and give us the strength. In Your Name we pray. Amen.

<u>S.A.I.L.O.R.S. On The Shore</u>

"**Nov. 4:** U.S. Defense Secretary Donald Rumsfeld discusses a dramatic enlargement of U.S. troops to be deployed in Central Asia with leaders from Uzbekistan and Tajikistan during weekend talks. Amr Moussa, the Secretary-General of the Arab League denounces bin Laden's TV statement, saying he 'does not speak in the name of Arabs and Muslims.' Egypt's Foreign Minister described bin Laden as being at war with the 'whole world.'

Nov. 5: Rumsfeld disclosed that U.S. helicopters had rescued Hamid Karzai. Anthrax is found in a Pentagon post office." *September11 News.com*

"Serve the Lord with gladness: come before His presence with singing." *Psalm 100:2 NKJV*

"In the Seoul Olympics, sailing competitions were under way at Pusan on September 24, 1988, with winds raging at 35 knots and playing havoc with the boats. Two sailors of the Singapore team, Joseph Chan and Shaw Her, were thrown overboard when their boat capsized.

Canada's Lawrence Lemieux was sailing alone nearby in a separate event when he saw the sailors in distress. He rescued Chan, who was exhausted from struggling against the strong currents in his weighted sailing jacket. By the time Lemieux finished helping the Singapore team, he had fallen well behind in his race.

Judges awarded Lemieux second place—the position he was in when he went to the sailors' aid—and the International Olympic Committee gave him a special award for his gallantry.

"It's the first rule of sailing to help people in distress," said Lemieux, downplaying the incident." – *Bud Greenspan in Parade*

- **S**ervice provided on land and sea

- **A**lert and ready to help with liberty

- **I**nspiring others towards victory

- **L**eading to protect a part of history

- **O**n shores to confirm the mystery

- **R**eady to help us reach our destiny

- Serving by being the best they can be.

Prayer: Heavenly Father, this day we ask that You will help us to see the needs around us as we endeavor to serve God and country. Let us see how the opportunities You present are often times to verify our love for those You placed in our lives. Let our eyes be opened, our hearts be challenged and our innermost selves be willing to reach out and lend a helping hand, not looking for glory or any type of recognition, simply done in order to represent You to our world. Amen.

C.O.A.S.T. Guard Patrols

"**NOV 6:** Germany commits 3,900 soldiers to the war on terrorism. The Northern Alliance claims the capture of strategic areas near the northern Afghanistan city of Mazar-e-Sharif. The FBI says the intelligence behind the warnings that terrorists might attack U.S. West Coast bridges was not credible." *September11News.com*

"Grace and peace to you from God our Father and the Lord Jesus Christ. Praise be to the God and Father of our Lord Jesus Christ. God is the Father who is full of mercy and all comfort. He comforts us every time we have trouble, so when others have trouble, we can comfort them with the same comfort God gives us." *2 Corinthians 1:2-4 NCV*

"There is the story of a young man who was kayaking off the coast of New England, in some very treacherous waters. He capsized and was being swept out to ocean. He did not have the power to fight the current, but he was able to pull his cell phone out of his pocket and call his father for help.

It didn't dawn on him that his father was over 3,000 miles away. His father called the nearest Coast Guard facility, and within twelve minutes, a Coast Guard Cutter was rescuing him.

That young man would tell the story to others of how he was saved because he called his father. And like that young man, when we get into serious trouble, most of us call our Father for help too, don't we?" *(sermoncentral.com/ill)*

Back home, the Coast Guard was patrolling around the outskirts of New York City on a daily basis. Occasionally they would arrange to come to shore and take some of the guards on a tour of the area, giving them a chance to see the situation from a different perspective. They were a constant source of reliability for outer protection, playing the role of a protecting father.

- **C**hosen for their skilled specialties,

- **O**n our many streams and waterways.

- **A**ttached to help with our current realities.

- Serving throughout these troubled days,

- Trying to comfort during these absurdities.

"A young man had grown to make his father very proud as a successful accountant, until one day he was arrested for embezzling. In the courtroom, this young man seemed unconcerned and unaffected by the charges. But when he was told to rise for his sentencing, his father stood as well. At that, the young man was crushed with shame and guilt for what he had done; a father had taken responsibility for the moral failure of his son." (SermonCentral.com/illustrations)

Prayer: Responsibility is a word for this day, as we look at those who serve the coast line of our country, as we look at the role of a father and son, as we look at our own lives as people chosen for our skills. Help us learn to be accountable and responsible, in prayer and support, as we endeavor to serve God and country. Amen.

Coast G.U.A.R.D. Patrols

"**Nov. 7:** British PM Tony Blair flies on the Concorde and meets with U.S. President George W. Bush. At a Washington press conference Blair says, 'the strategy has to encompass more than air strikes...there are other operations we will mount.' Bush added, 'slowly but surely the Taliban is crumbling.' A 911 call from a dying postal worker is released." *September11News.com*

"Put on the full armor of God, that you may be able to stand against the tricks of the devil." *Ephesians 6:11 CEB*

The Army, Navy, Marines, Coast Guard and the Air Force all had representatives serving in differing capacities during 9/11. All had their memories and their stories to tell. Some were wonderful to hear, some brought dread and fear, some brought joy and cheer. Then there were some that would never to be repeated.

Several stories I was hearing at present had to do with guarding or being guarded by another service member or by their God. I remember standing joyfully observing on shoreline at a guard point with a couple soldiers at one of the Nuclear Plants. We watched, saluted and waved at the personnel on a Coast Guard vessel providing outer bank security while patrolling the area.

This event reminded me of story I had read: "A soldier explains how a song sung by an enemy changed him. One Christmas Eve, Ira D. Sankey was traveling by steamboat up the Delaware River. Asked to sing, Mr. Sankey sang the "Shepherd Song." After the song was ended, a man with a rough, weather-beaten face came up to Mr. Sankey and said: "Did you ever serve in the Union Army?" Sankey replied "Yes, I did, in the spring of 1860." The man asked, "Can you remember if you were doing picket duty on a bright moonlight night in 1862?" Sankey was surprised and said, "Yes, I did." The stranger said, "So did I. But I was serving in the Confederate army.

When I saw you standing at your post I said to myself: 'That fellow will never get away from here alive.' I raised my musket and took aim. I was standing in the shadow completely concealed, while the full light of the moon was falling upon you. At that instant, just as a moment ago, you raised your eyes to Heaven and began to sing. Music, especially song, has always had a wonderful power over me, and I took my finger off the trigger. 'Let him sing his song to the end' I said to myself. 'I can shoot him afterwards. He's my victim at all events, and my bullet cannot miss him.' But the song you sang then was the song you sang just now. I heard the words perfectly:

We are You, do You befriend us. Be the guardian of our way.

Those words stirred up many memories in my heart. I began to think of my childhood and my God-fearing mother. She had many, many times sung that song to me. But she died all too soon, otherwise much in my life would no doubt have been different. When you had finished your song it was impossible for me to take aim at you again. I thought: 'The Lord who is able to save that man from certain death must surely be great and mighty,' and my arm of its own accord dropped limp at my side." – *From Religious Digest, reported in Encyclopedia of 7700 Illustrations, Paul Lee Tan*

- **G**rant comfort in God's election

- **U**ndergird with Divine Selection

- **A**llow Godly wisdom for direction

- **R**escue through Your protection

- **D**eliver with the power of Your correction

Prayer: Lord, I thank You, for those who have chosen to guard our homes, land and country. I also thank You for all You have done to protect us over the years in the times of needed protection, both personal and spiritually. I ask You for Your divine selection, wisdom and direction, that it may be passed on to all who desire to rejoice in it. Lord, we need your love, strength, and power, especially during the times You offer Your correction. Guard our decisions and let each bring honor to You. Amen.

A.I.R.M.E.N. Guide

"**Nov. 8:** U.S. air strikes reportedly kill 85 Islamic militants and a Taliban commander near Mazar-e-Sharif. U.S. commander, General Tommy Franks, said a 'big fight' was continuing for the strategic northern stronghold. The fall of Mazar, with its supply routes and large airfield, could trigger the arrival of U.S. ground forces for a northern bridgehead. President Bush tours the Center for Disease Control (CDC) in Atlanta, and in a nationally televised speech, he said, 'This great nation will never be intimidated.' Bush closed with, 'My fellow Americans, let's roll.'" *September11News.com*

"Fulfill My joy, that you be likeminded, having the same love, being of one accord, and one mind." *Philippians 2:2 NKJV*

Like most people who serve within a command, we had regular staff calls with continuing discussion of the military situation and where we fit in. I had my first encounter, within the 9/11 framework, with our fellow service members of the Air Force during this crisis, when I went with a number of the leaders to a gathering of security forces. The lead General at the Air Force base within proximity of the disaster gave an excellent briefing on what each branch was doing for security. The General also discussed with others and me about developing further Critical Incident Stress Debriefing (CSID) teams along with how and where we needed to introduce these services providing aid to struggling service members across the multitude of branches.

We are grateful for all Airmen:

- At duty stations they take a stand,

- Involved in guarding our precious land.

- Ready to give life if need be,

- Men and women of true dignity.

- Enlist them into our time of prayer,

- Noting unity – showing we all care.

Prayer: Lord, there are so many who served in so many different ways during our time of shared and personal crisis. We thank you for all ranks of service members, from the generals to the privates, each who had their specific duties to perform. Thank you for those who have to make the decisions and those who willingly follow their orders. Help us to continually pray for our service members who served then and still serve today. Amen.

N.O.W. Serving

"**Nov. 9:** In the biggest victory of the month-long war, anti-Taliban forces capture the northern Afghan city of Mazar-e-Sharif. Taliban officials in Kabul confirmed they had lost control of the strategic city. President Bush meets with Indian PM Vajpayee in Washington. Anthrax spores are found in four New Jersey postal facilities." *September11News.com*

"Be strong and courageous, because you will lead these people to inherit the land I swore to their forefathers to give them." *Joshua 1:6 (NIV)*

The urgency of the day was seen throughout the service branches during 9/11. FEMA was there to give us the daily updates regarding where the needs were. Each person received their assignments, and I received updated situations or personal needs information, to verify where I could be of greatest assistance. Red Cross was there also, to provide on a different level. The community was doing all it could, but there were still greater needs they could not meet, without the help of an authoritative voice. Many of these specialized people travel from one location to another and are still now serving in locations throughout the world.

I wish to share the words of former President Theodore Roosevelt toward those who were now serving: "A man who is good enough to shed his blood for his country is good enough to be given a square deal afterwards. More than that no man is entitled, and less than that no man shall have." – *(Speech to veterans, Springfield, IL, July 4, 1903.)*

- **N**ow is a time that continues forever here

- **O**ppressing, opposing, ordering no cheer

- **W**inning is an option, thru God, who is always near.

Mother Theresa emphasized:

"When I was hungry, you gave me food to eat.

When I was thirsty, you gave me your cup to drink.

Whatsoever you do to the least of these of my children,

that you do unto me.

Now enter the house of my Father.

When I was homeless, you opened your doors.

When I was naked, you gave me your coat.

When I was weary, you helped me find rest.

When I was anxious, you calmed my fears.

When I was little, you taught me to read.

When I was lonely, you gave me your love.

When I was in prison, you came to my cell.

When on a sick bed, you cared for my needs.

In a strange country, you made me at home.

Seeking employment, you found me a job.

Hurt in a battle, you bound up my wounds.

Searching for kindness, you held out your hand.

When I was a Negro or Chinese or White,

Mocked and insulted you carried my cross.

When I was aged, you bothered to smile.

When I was restless, you listened and cared.

You saw me covered with spittle and blood,

You knew my features, though grimy with sweat.

When I was laughed at, you stood by my side.

When I was happy, you shared in my joy."

Prayer: Heavenly Father, I pray for all the individuals who came forward for help during our CISD briefings, knowing their desire for additional personal help and sometimes misunderstood help from You. Lord help us be encouraged through a prayer written by Ted Loder: "Empower me to be a bold participant, rather than a timid saint in waiting; to exercise authority of honesty, rather than to defer to power or deceive to get it; to influence someone for justice, rather than impress anyone for gain; and by grace, to find treasures of joy, of friendship, of peace hidden in the fields you give me daily to plow." – *(Ted Loder, Life Prayers)*

Heavenly Father, help us be willing to now serve, being more than a person dealing with critical incident stress. Help us be persons who no longer need a debriefing to live in peace, but a people living in the peace of Your Glory. Amen.

Now S.E.R.V.I.N.G.

"Nov 10: President Bush tells the UN that all countries share an urgent obligation to battle terrorism. "For every regime that sponsors terror, there is a price to be paid and it will be paid ... the time for action has now arrived." After receiving a scolding from Saudi Arabia,

Bush continues to reject a meeting with Yasser Arafat while the two are in New York for Bush's UN address. Pakistan's largest newspaper publishes an interview with Osama bin Laden. "If America used chemical and nuclear weapons against us, then we may retort with chemical and nuclear weapons. We have the weapons as a deterrent," claims bin Laden.

Nov. 11: Leaders of several countries join U.N. Secretary General Kofi Annan and President George W. Bush for a memorial service honoring countries who had casualties in the WTC attacks. The two month anniversary of the September 11 attacks falls on a day most of the western world remembers their war veterans (U.S. - Veterans Day, Canada/UK – Remembrance Day)." *September11News.com*

"Serve the LORD with reverent fear, and rejoice with trembling." *Psalm 2:11 NLT*

I joined the troops, as today's news caused some increased tensions for service members looking forward, because it looked like we were taking two steps backwards. Many feared being pulled from their assignment here to being sent overseas. At this point, most preferred to remain near family and friends, to continue rebuilding their homes and reestablishing their routines.

I found that I had mixed feelings and prayed that I would be where I was needed. My prayer was, "Would You direct me please."

In the midst of questions and uncertainties, God introduced a night that proved to be a little different than usual. This night, as my assistant and I were finishing the night shift, we came upon a hooker who was talking with a policeman – she appeared slightly drunk. As she walked away from the police officer, she flashed us, with her upper torso. The policeman simply smiled and walked away; I joined him smiling and walking away.

Those who were currently serving continued to face similar temptations and struggles that affected their, physical, emotional and spiritual state, especially when their service took them to places away from home. For some who spent their whole life in New York City, presently being at home was just as difficult.

"There are a good many problems before the American people today and before me as president, but I expect to find the solution to those problems just in the proportion that I am faithful in the study of the Word of God." – *Woodrow Wilson, American Statesman, 1782-1852*

The answers come down to being a person who is serving, knowing God is working, and help is readily available to the individuals who studying His word for wisdom, encouragement, comfort and continuous fortitude:

- **S**earch and see if you can find

- **E**very place that God does not mind

- **R**esponding to our individual times.

- **V**oices from the past give us our signs

- **I**nspection will verify God led the way.

- **N**ever once did God actually turn away,

- **G**o to Him with what you have to say.

Prayer: Heavenly Father, let us be grateful for all the opportunities to serve that You bring our way. Help us to read Your Word and apply it to our lives that we might gladly serve and rejoice. Lord, show us ourselves, and help us know ourselves, in order that we might be ones who are willing to serve in special ways that honor You. We are weak and You are strong. Help us rely on Your strength while joyfully serving. Amen.

Chapter 7

Deliverance Was Asked (43-50)

". . . help them to be safe from harm."

He refreshes and restores my life (myself). *Psalm 23:3a AMP*

"A Christian railroad engineer was speaking to a group of fellow workers about heaven. He said, "I can't begin to tell you what the Lord Jesus means to me. In Him I have a hope that is very precious. Let me explain.

Many years ago as each night I neared the end of my run, I would always let out a long blast with the whistle just as I'd come around the last curve. Then I'd look up at the familiar little cottage on top of the hill. My mother and father would be standing in the doorway waving to me. After I had passed, they'd go back inside and say, 'Thank God, Benny is home safe again tonight.' Well, they are gone now, and no one is there to welcome me. But someday when I have finished my 'earthly run' and I draw near to heaven's gate, I believe I'll see my precious mother and dad waiting there for me. And the one will turn to the other and say, 'Thank God, Benny is home safe at last.'" *From Bible.org*

H.E.L.P. Them

Nov. 12: "American Airlines <u>Flight 587 </u>flying from NYC's Kennedy Airport to the Dominican Republic crashes into a residential neighborhood in Queens, N.Y., only minutes after takeoff. All 260 passengers and crew are killed, and six people on the ground are missing. Flight 587 left the airport at 9:14 A.M., over 70 minutes late. The early indications lead NTSB investigators to announce the likely cause was mechanical failure, and not another act of airline terrorism. Eyewitnesses say that the engines and other plane parts appeared to have exploded and then fell off prior to the crash. The engines are found blocks from the main crash site, and the tail section is retrieved from the waters in Jamaican Bay. President Bush tells the American people, 'New York people have suffered mightily, they suffer again, but there is no doubt in my mind that New Yorkers are resilient and strong and courageous people and will help their neighbors overcome this recent incident.' When NY Mayor Giuliani heard of the plane crash he said, 'Oh, my God. We are just being tested one more time, and we are going to pass this test too.' Ironically the plane crashed into a neighborhood where many firefighters and policemen lived, and who were involved in the September 11th WTC rescue efforts. The community where Flight 587 crashed had already lost over 70 people in the WTC attack weeks before." *September11News.com*

"I will lift up my eyes unto the hills, from where comes my help."
Psalm 121:1 NASB

Sorrow again gripped the air as death left its mark, and the shadow spread gloom once again near the valley of death known as the Twin Towers. The loss and destruction from another plane: was it an accident or another plot?

Many looked up that night as we heard the engines of a plane that seemed awfully close. The guard post I was visiting by the shoreline at Ground Zero, saw the not-so-distant bright lights, and then heard what sounded like a massive explosion; adrenalin levels reached renewed heights. The speculation started bubbling over with many differing thoughts about what had just happened. It seemed like an eternity before the word was passed down the line about what really transpired.

Many who were serving in New York City that night knew people who were, once again, looking for family members amidst the scattered plane parts and destroyed property, hoping upon hope that they would hear good news knowing there was nothing more they could do except wait.

I found it a disheartening journey through the shadow of death that night. I was constantly reminded of the past cloud of darkness, as I drove around the city seeing the diminishing remains of the temporary monuments of pictures, letters, poetry, and wishes from 9/11. Here the island was facing a whole new crisis.

The soldiers, who were sitting or standing at their position of guardianship, again became active listening posts for many different city residents. They were again being asked by those passing by "what do I do now" or "why again?" They in turn would ask the Chaplain, "What do I say?" I would tell them I don't have all the answers nor will I pretend to therefore I would then refer them to passages similar to Psalm 121;1-2 "I will lift up my eyes to the mountains. Where will my help come from? My help comes from the Lord, Who made heaven and earth. (NLV)

It was during of these times I once again looked up and requested, "Lord, give me the words to say, the ears to hear and the heart to share and help these people find the inner peace, the personal comfort, the spiritual guidance, that comes only from You."

I would remind service-members of the truth. The truth was they had to wait with uncertainty, wait with never-ending hope, and wait with friends and family. I could offer encouragement to them, but I along with them had to wait upon God. True, the events and loss of lives does not make sense. Personally, I still believe God in charge and still cares, even though for many that seems so untrue.

"During the course of his sermon, a preacher wanted to emphasize the brevity of life. He took a long pause, then said, 'Every member of this church is going to die.' But, to his ultimate surprise, a man in the back row responded to this statement with a big smile.

Well, the evangelist was stunned, so he repeated the phrase with even greater volume. This time he noticed that the man crossed his arms and looked even happier than before. Well, this rattled the preacher so much that he literally shouted the words a third time at the top of his lungs, 'Every member of this church is going to die!'

But, in the midst of a loud but serious cry of 'Amen's' from the congregation, that guy in the back seat just kept beaming from ear to ear. Well immediately after the service, the evangelist tracked down the man and asked, 'Why in the world did you smile so big when I said 'Every member of this church is going to die?'' The man erupted with a huge smile and said, 'Because I'm not a member of this church.'" – *Unknown (sermoncentral.com/ill)*

The events of 9/11 and of this evening once again reminded me of the many who died. We do not know the day or the hour, but we do need to be ready whether we are a member of the same faith or not. The service members still were questioning what had transpired on 9/11 and now this! My point was the same as the pastor in the previous illustration: are we ready?

Prayer: Lord, once again another tragedy has occurred, and we question our security as we once again see the shadow of death in our presence.

- **H**ear our prayers – Lord this day

- **E**nliven us with Your love within.

- **L**ift us into Your light's awesome ray

- **P**lease help us this day to see You win.

It is true Lord, today's events may cause us to stumble in our faith because of the uncertainty of what transpired. Let our inner strength and victory, which comes from You, overcome our apparent loss. Thank you, Lord. Amen.

Help T.H.E.M.

"**Nov. 14:** In the haste of the Al-Qaeda departure from Kabul, documents are left behind clearly indicating Osama bin Laden's network is actively attempting to develop nuclear devices. …. The investigators of the crash of Flight 587 suspect that the plane took off sooner than approved and may have been caught in the 'wake turbulence' of another plane. U.S. President Bush plays host to President Putin at Bush's 640-hectare Prairie Chapel Ranch in Crawford Texas." *September11News.com*

"I used to think that God's gifts were on shelves one above another, and the taller we grow, the easier we can reach them. Now I find, that God's gifts are on shelves one beneath another, and the lower we stoop, the more we get." *F. B. Meyer.*

"Humble yourselves, under the mighty hand of God, that He may exalt you at the proper time, casting all your cares upon Him, because He cares for you." *1 Peter 5:6-7 ASV*

To humble ourselves is a difficult task for a service member, *actually for anyone,* because we are taught to stand tall and have been trained to think we can handle any situation. The experience service members were now dealing with in New York City was not a common occurrence. This was very humbling, because it happened in their country, and for some, on their homes. Words of encouragement were often needed and were frequently offered.

- This is the day – A gift from above.

- Help us to fill each moment with love.

- Everyone occasionally needs extra care.

- Make me willing to receive and share.

A. W. Tozer wrote, "I have met two classes of Christians: the proud who imagine that they are humble, and the humble who are afraid to be proud. There should be a third class: the self-forgetful who leave the whole thing in the hands of Christ and refuse to waste any time trying to make themselves good and humble. They will reach the goal far ahead of the rest of us."

Local duty, beyond weekend drills, for our service members was something new and somewhat terrifying. They, like most of the world, needed to learn our God does care for them, and He needed to let this hurting world around them know to trust the love of God.

Prayer: Heavenly Father, we look at the situation and find it hard to be humble. We want to take charge. We want to exact revenge. We want to make things right. Help us Lord learn to cast – throw – heave – dump ALL our cares upon You. Amen.

T.O. B.E. Safe

"**Nov. 15**: Eight aid workers, held captive in Afghanistan since August for teaching Christianity, are flown to Pakistan by U.S. Special Forces after being abandoned by the fleeing Taliban. The captives feared the Taliban were preparing for their executions, and called their rescue 'a miracle.' Russian President Putin flies to New York and tours Ground Zero with NY Mayor Giuliani. Colin Powell agrees to get involved in Middle East peace talks. Flight 587 investigators say the flight data recorder indicates the A300 jet had two 'wake encounters' during the three-minute flight." *September11News.com*

"Let the words of my mouth and the meditation of my heart be acceptable in your sight. O Lord My Rock and My Redeemer." *Psalm 19:14 AMP*

Service members again were questioning the words to use in response to the questions of those who stopped to say hello.

"Unfortunately, the words we use don't always have the effect we want. Sometimes words meant to spur people on toward action, fall on deaf ears and immobile people. Sometimes the words we use to encourage are interpreted as patronizing or condescending. Sometimes we don't know what words to use, and we choose ones that end up doing more harm than good." *(Sermon: "The Words of My Mouth" by Bryan Dill)*

How often I am reminded of Mel Brook's movie, *To Be or Not to Be.*

- **To** be the person You want me to be

- **Only** You can help me be this way.

- **Begin** with the next person I see

- **Enable** them by the words I say.

An interesting story about wrong words written by Laura Schlessinger *(The Ten Commandments: The Significance of God's Laws in Everyday Life*, p. 203) follows:

"My name is Gossip. I have no respect for justice. I maim without killing. I break hearts and ruin lives. I am cunning and malicious and gather strength with age. The more I am quoted, the more I am believed. I flourish at every level of society. My victims are helpless. They cannot protect themselves against me because I have no face. To track me down is impossible. The harder you try, the more elusive I become. I am nobodies' friend. Once I tarnish a reputation, it is never the same. I topple governments, wreck marriages, and ruin careers – cause sleepless nights, heartaches, and indigestion. I spawn suspicion and generate grief. I make innocent people cry in their pillows. Even my name hisses. I make headlines and headaches. Before you repeat a story, ask yourself, Is it true? Is it fair? Is it necessary? If not – shut up!"

Matthew 12:36 says, "I tell you, on the day of judgment, people will give account for every careless word they speak." (HCSB)

Prayer: I come today, Lord, to ask that the words of those who choose to follow will not be idle or vicious and bring judgment upon us. I pray that the words spoken will be chosen in Godly love and direction. Lord let our words touch, not pierce the heart. Give us the ability to humbly speak words that are acceptable in Your sight. Amen.

To Be S.A.F.E.

"**Nov 16:** U.S. air strikes reportedly killed Mohammed Atef, a key lieutenant to Osama bin Laden and the al-Qaeda network. The U.S. Congress approves a federal takeover of air security, and National Guard troops will soon screen bags until mandated screening machines arrive." *September11News.com*

The idea of safety continues; one night the service members assisted the police in arresting a soldier impersonating a CID person at the World Trade Center (WTC), and another night they helped catch some looters at WTC. There was a continuing flow of individuals who wanted to cheat, steal, and gain access to places where they were not supposed to be. There are still many today who are trying to rob us of our individual peace.

"Peace I leave with you; my peace I give to you. Not as the world gives do I give to you. Let not your hearts be troubled, neither let them be afraid*" John 14:27 NEV*

Where does true peace come from? Jesus tells us, "In Me you may have peace; in this world you will have trouble. But take heart! I have overcome the world" (John 16:33). *Today's New International Version.*

Charles Spurgeon wrote, "God cannot give us peace apart from Himself, for it is not there. There is no such thing."

Thomas Merton writes, "Man is not at peace with his fellow man because he is not at peace with himself. He is not at peace with himself, because he is not at peace with God."

Time has passed and still many are looking for some sort of peace. The shadow of death still lingers with an overbearing presence. They no longer feel safe in their own home area.

- Secure within the arms of love,

- And comforted from support above.

- Finding God will gently shove

- Each toward that peace, like a dove.

"During the Korean War, a young Marine lay dying on Heartbreak Ridge. A chaplain came to him and whispered, "Can I help you, son?" The Marine replied, "No sir, it's all right." The Chaplain then saw the source of this dying Marine's peace. He was clutching a small New Testament in his bloody hand, and his finger was placed on the assurance of John 14:27: *"My peace I give to you." Sermoncentral.com /illustrations*

Prayer: Lord, I too want live in the peace that only You can give. With Your help, we can begin once again to feel safe at home, because we know You are there. We know You will guide us through the shadows. Grant Your peace this day and let me rest in it. Amen.

Safe F.R.O.M. Harm

"**Nov 17:** Laura Bush spoke in place of U.S. President Bush for the weekly White House radio address. The First Lady said the war was 'a fight for the rights and dignity of women.'

Nov 18: The planned deployment of a full brigade of British troops in Afghanistan stays in doubt as the Northern Alliance continue to disagree with the role of foreign troops.

Nov 19: Four international journalists are ambushed and killed by gunmen in a mountain pass on the road to Kabul. A Kabul movie theater opens for the first time in five years. U.S. President George W. Bush signs the new air security bill federalizing airport inspectors." *September11News.com*

"But let all who take refuge in you be glad; let them ever sing for joy. Spread your protection over them that those who love your name may rejoice in you." *Psalm 5:11 (NIV)*

Some veterans bear visible signs of their service: a missing limb, a jagged scar, a certain look in the eye. Others may carry the evidence inside them: a pin holding a bone together, a piece of shrapnel in the leg. I find myself, like several military, dealing with personal reminders such as malaria, Agent Orange, blood agents, and unknown ailments that have arisen from prior service assignments and 9/11. These wounds remain hidden for the rest of our lives. Except in parades or on days when we honor our vets, these men and women who have kept America safe from harm wear no badge or emblem.

Traveling to other military sites, such as West Point, the vigilant role of protection was also evident. They would make you open your hood, open your trunk, and ask you to get out of the car, while they ran mirrors under your vehicle. Even though I knew I had done nothing wrong, I felt guilty. However, I accepted their activities, because I knew the concept was to keep all personnel safe from harm.

Let our safety be found in God:

- From now on help me to voice

- Right from wrong, lest I lose

- Open my eyes – don't let me snooze

- May Your Love be my final choice

The courage of Civil War leader Stonewall Jackson in the midst of conflict can be a lesson for the believer.

Historian Mark Brimsley wrote:

"A battlefield is a deadly place, even for generals; and it would be naive to suppose Jackson never felt the animal fear of all beings exposed to wounds and death. But invariably, he displayed extraordinary calm under fire; a calm too deep and masterful to be mere pretense. His apparent obliviousness to danger attracted notice, and after the First Manassas battle, someone asked him how he managed it. 'My religious belief teaches me to feel as safe in battle as in bed,' Jackson explained. 'God knows the time for my death. I do not concern myself about that, but to be always ready, no matter where it may overtake me.' He added pointedly, 'That is the way all men should live, and then all would be equally brave.'"

Prayer: Lord, once again we speak about the calmness and comfort that comes from knowing Your peace. Help me and others with our choices towards You. Let us learn to seek and speak boldly about a type of peace that can be found only in You. For this I am truly grateful, Lord. Amen.

Safe From H.A.R.M.

"**Nov. 20:** At a conference in Washington, attended by 21 countries to discuss the reconstruction of Afghanistan, Colin Powell said, 'We are going to have an enormous obligation to not leave the Afghan people in the lurch, and not walk away as has been done in the past.' The

Pentagon moves hundreds more U.S. Marines on amphibious vessels to the region to help in the hunt for Osama bin Laden. The U.S. military drops leaflets into Afghanistan offering a $25 million reward for Osama bin Laden and his associates." *September11News.com*

"Celebrate God all day, every day. I mean, revel in him! Make it as clear as you can to all you meet that you're on their side, working with them and not against them. Help them see that the Master is about to arrive. He could show up any minute! Don't fret or worry. Instead of worrying, pray. Let petitions and praises shape your worries into prayers, letting God know your concerns. Before you know it, a sense of God's wholeness, everything coming together for good, will come and settle you down. It's wonderful what happens when Christ displaces worry at the center of your life. *Philippians 4:4-6 MSG*

"In, *The Horse Whisperer*, Tom Booker has a gift when it comes to what he calls "gentling" horses. In one telling scene, a traumatized horse frightened by a ringing cell phone, gallops off into the far end of a large pasture. Booker walks into the pasture and sits down, where he waits for what appears to be hours. Drawn by curiosity, the horse inches closer and closer, finally allowing itself to be touched by the "whisperer," who leads it back to the safety of its stall. Like that horse, there are a lot of people who need a gentle touch and voice. Life and people have handed them situations which have spooked them and caused them to run off seeking a "safe" place. Yet in reality, the only "safety" can be found in God, whose love is constant." (Illustrations – Sermoncentral.com)

For many military personnel the fear never really goes away from service in a combat zone, and I anticipate the same occurred after serving in the terrorist zone. Years may pass, but the inner fear hangs on, being triggered by a picture, an activity or an event. New York City was not the site of a war; however, the memories of 9/11 continue to cause internal struggles for many. Struggles not expressed, sometimes not even identified, continue to haunt some of those brave military, first responders and volunteers who gave of themselves tirelessly.

Prayer: Today, Lord, we ask that you help us lift those who struggle with a lack of peace and ongoing fear of the shadows. Enable them to:

- Have a terrifically wonderful day.

- Accept the blessings God sends their way.

- Receive the words He, with love, does say.

- May it be a day of beautiful glorious array!

"So we can say for sure, "The Lord is my Helper. I am not afraid of anything man can do to me." Hebrews 13:6 (NLV) Amen

Chapter 8

Your Presence Was Requested (51-56)

"Protect until battles have ceased."

P.R.O.T.E.C.T.

"**Nov. 21:** The U.S. Justice Department determines that all 19 hijackers in the Sept. 11 attacks entered the U.S. legally, on temporary visas issued at U.S. consulates in the Middle East and Europe. Speaking to 10,000 cheering U.S. paratroopers of the 101st Airborne in Fort Campbell Ky., U.S. President Bush said, 'Afghanistan is just the beginning on the war against terror. Across the world and across the years, we will fight these evil ones, and we will win.' Syed Tayyab Agha, the 28 year-old protégé of Supreme leader Mullah Mohammed Omar said, 'You should forget the Sept. 11 attacks because now there is new fighting against Islam. We hope mighty Allah will break America.' A 94-year-old Connecticut widow, who rarely left her home, becomes the fifth anthrax fatality." *September11 News.com*

"The reason why many fail in battle is because they wait until the hour of battle. The reason why others succeed is because they have gained their victory on their knees long before the battle came. Anticipate your battles; fight them on your knees before temptation comes, and you will always have victory." *Torrey, R.A.*

"I am with you always, even to the end of the age." *Matthew 28:20 (NIV)*

God does desire to protect those who serve. *I believe He must have a special angel assigned to those who have to drive in the city on a daily basis.* I had a military vehicle which gave me priority travel, entrance and parking, but I will admit my prayer life increased greatly while I served in New York City following the events of 9/11, especially when I had to drive myself through the city during the day time. Night-time driving was nowhere near as bad. I sure missed my assistant when he got reassigned and I had to drive myself. You had to be there, but believe me: most people who do not live in the big city could not imagine what this type of driving was like. At least when I was in Korea, I knew that it was standard for drivers to make five lanes of traffic out of a three-lane highway.

God protects in unusual ways. The following story illustrates:

"The only survivor of a shipwreck was washed-up on a small uninhabited island. He prayed feverishly for God to rescue him, and every day he scanned the horizon for help, but none seemed forthcoming.

Exhausted, he eventually managed to build a little hut out of driftwood, to protect him from the elements and to store his few possessions.

But then one day after scavenging for food, he arrived home to find his little hut in flames, the smoke billowing up to the sky. The worst had happened; everything was lost. He was stung with grief and anger. 'God, how could you do this to me!' he cried.

Early the next day, however, he was awakened by the sound of a ship that was approaching the island. It had come to rescue him. 'How did you know I was here?' asked the weary man of his rescuers.

'We saw your smoke signal,' they replied." *(Christianstories.com)*

Prayer: Our Heavenly Father today we thank You for Your Son and

- **P**ray for Your divine protection as You

- **R**each out with powerful loving arms to each

- **O**ne of us by giving: individual strength and support;

- **T**ouching our hearts with Your genuine compassion;

- **E**ncouraging us to work toward a possible peace;

- **C**herishing our efforts to live and love Your plan and

- **T**eaching that You are always there for us. Thank you, Lord. Amen.

U.N.T.I.L.

"**Nov 22:** The Alliance responded with a barrage of long-range rockets. As Americans welcome Thanksgiving Day, U.S. forces continue to bomb Taliban front line positions in Konduz." *September11News.com*

"If any of you need wisdom, ask God for it. He will give it to you. God gives freely to everyone. He doesn't find fault." *James 1:5 NIRV*

Time has passed, and many are still looking for answers within their own minds and lives. The questions never really stopped throughout the tour of duty at the site of 9/11, as service members questioned the need for them to be there. They were reaching a point mid-tour believing that their service had become redundant and meaningless, since danger no longer seemed imminent. A few had settled in, but many, especially those who had a job to go back to, were ready to return home and start over. It was not a matter of wisdom for them, but it was the wisdom of the military to detain them longer. Regrettably, there were many who were still not really thankful this Thanksgiving season.

God's wisdom is Divine, compared to mankind's wisdom identified in some of the following examples:

1. "Everything that can be invented has been invented." – *Charles H. Duell, Commissioner, U.S. Office of Patents, 1899*

2. "We went to Atari and said, 'Hey, we've got this amazing thing, even built with some of your parts, and what do you think about funding us? Or we'll give it to you. We just want to do it. Pay our salary; we will come to work for you.' And they said, 'No.' So then we went to Hewlett-Packard, and they said, 'Hey, we don't need you. You haven't gotten through college yet.'" – *Apple Computer Inc. founder Steve Jobs, on attempts to get Atari and H-P interested in his and Steve Wozniak's personal computer.*

3. "I will have nothing to do with a God who cares only occasionally. I need a God who is with us always, everywhere, in the deepest depths as well as the highest heights. It is when things go wrong, when good things do not happen, when our prayers seem to have been lost, that God is most present. We do not need the sheltering wings when things go smoothly. We are closest to God in the darkness, stumbling along blindly." – *Madeleine L'Engle*

We as individuals need to offer this prayer for wisdom: Lord,

- **U**tilize me for Your benefit I pray.

- **N**udge me, as I need it, along the way.

- **T**ell me what I personally can do this day.

- **I**llumine me with Your Wisdom Divine.

- Let Your Love through me continually shine. Amen.

B.A.T.T.L.E.S. Have Not Ceased

"**Nov 24:** According to U.K. news sources, British paratroopers are on 48-hours notice, and will join some 25,000 elite American paratroopers from the 101st and 82nd Airborne Divisions, who intend to encircle the city of Kandahar

Nov. 25: Foreign Taliban prisoners overpower their Northern Alliance guards at a prison near Mazar-e-Sharif, triggering a fierce gun battle that killed hundreds and was put down only after U.S. air and ground forces were called in

Nov. 26: Tapes are released revealing the last minutes of Flight 93. The hijackers are heard screaming at each other while the sounds of plates and metal trays crash repeatedly against the cockpit door. The hijacker at the controls tried to knock the passengers off their feet by putting the plane into a steep dive. Flight 93 crashed into a field in Pennsylvania after the hijackers were rushed by heroes aboard the flight." *September 11News.com*

"Do everything readily and cheerfully – no bickering, no second-guessing allowed! Go out into the world uncorrupted, a breath of fresh air in this squalid and polluted society. Provide people with a glimpse of good living and of the living God. Carry the light-giving message into the night, so I'll have good cause to be proud of you on the day that Christ returns. You'll be living proof that I didn't go to all this work for nothing." *Philippians 2:14-16 (MSG)*

Our Thanksgiving has been over a very short while, and life has returned to normal. As much as we long for peace, we see our military battles have not ceased, and our personal battles continue as we hear the black box recording from Flight 93 opening up old wounds and concerns for those who tediously sat watching into the night.

I believe former President LBJ gave us a good thought to reflect on today: "If we fail now, then we will have forgotten in abundance what we learned in hardship: that democracy rests on faith; freedom asks more than it gives; and the judgment of God is harshest on those who are most favored." *– Lyndon Baines Johnson, Inaugural Address, 1965*

As I look back over many years of varied military service, I vividly remember the moment when I first encountered today's verse from Philippians 2. I was in Basic Training, January 1966, Fort Dix, NJ. This verse helped me get through, because I knew that "All things were possible with God" but did not understand why I was where I was at this time in my life. What hit home the most was the phrase: *Do everything readily and cheerfully—no bickering, no second-guessing allowed!* – The King James Version said: "Do all things without complaining and disputing." This was a difficult concept for me to accept as a teenager in Basic Training. I found many of my military counterparts were very good at complaining and disputing. It was a part of their normal lifestyle. Imagine if all of us could learn to live without murmuring and complaining. This verse helped me develop my basic attitude for life as a child of God: "Praise the Lord."

Have you ever heard of Lieutenant Hirro Onada? He was the last Japanese soldier to surrender after World War II. He was left on the island Lubang in the Philippines in 1944 along with three other soldiers. They were left with the command to "carry on the mission even if Japan surrenders." Eventually the others were killed or surrendered. But Onada continued his war alone.

Through the years, he ignored messages from loudspeakers announcing Japan's surrender. Leaflets were dropped in the jungle begging him to surrender, so he could return to Japan. During his 29-year private war, he killed at least 30 Philippine nationals. More than half a million dollars was spent trying to locate him and convince him to surrender.

Finally, on March 10, 1974 Onada surrendered his rusty sword, after receiving a personal command from his former superior officer. His lonely war was finally over. When he returned to Japan as a prematurely aged man of 52, he made this comment: "Nothing pleasant during those 29 years in the jungle." *(Newsweek, 1974)*

Hirro's battles finally had ceased, but for some the aftermath of 9/11 and Flight 93 continues daily, causing anxious memories. The question for today is how do we deal with the battles we face? Are they ongoing or have they ceased?

- **B**attles come and bring all sorts of pain,

- **A**llowing God's Spirit to give strength to win.

- **T**ender is His love with much to claim,

- **T**hink of His presence to help you begin.

- **L**isten as God instructs again and again.

- **E**njoy guidance to help you with His love.

- **S**ing, since God offers help from above.

Prayer: Today we come to join together to pray for the battles of life. Some are very real, some are very deep, some are destructive while others bring healing. Lord, we ask for victorious battles that bring healing to all who call upon You this day. Give us the strength and armor to fight each battle. In Your name we pray. Amen.

Battles H.A.V.E. Not Ceased

"**Nov. 27:** In the bloodiest engagement of the war in Afghanistan, imprisoned foreign Taliban soldiers, in a mud-brick fort outside of

Mazar-e-Sharif, are all killed. The death toll includes scores of Northern Alliance soldiers and a CIA operative, who was questioning the Taliban at the time of the prison uprising on Nov. 25th." *September11News.com*

God stripped the spiritual rulers and powers of their authority. With the cross, he won the victory and showed the world that they were powerless. *Colossians 2:15 NCV*

Easter is long past, but it reminded us of one of the bloodiest events in the history of the world, and an event that proved to be the greatest victory for mankind.

Thanksgiving was here. It was not the time service members wanted to hear about one of bloodiest engagements of the war. However, those serving in the city and other points were glad they were not in the midst of those battles.

"History tells us: In the autumn of 1944, Germany had been beaten back behind its borders. The Nazi war machine was nearly destroyed. The repeated bombing raids of the Allies all but assured that Hitler's forces would never rise again. Around the perimeter of Germany's borders, the Allies spread a thin line of forces. One person observed that Allied forces were so scattered that a man could slip between its lines without being observed.

All across Europe, there was celebration rejoicing in Germany's defeat. The war was effectively over. The only problem was . . . somebody forgot to tell Germany.

Even as his forces were being shattered and driven back, Hitler was devising a plan for one last onslaught. Underground factories churned out more weapons, armament and ammunition. More of Germany's young and old men were conscripted and trained for war. And as Europe rejoiced, Hitler planned.

Hitler's goal was not to drive back the Allies into the sea, as much as it was to divide the British to the North and Americans to the South, so demoralizing them that they would seek peace on his terms and not theirs.

On Dec. 16, 1944 Hitler's army began The Ardennes Offensive, also known as The Battle of the Bulge. Over 1,000,000 men fought along an 85-mile front; when the fighting ended Jan. 25, 1945 hundreds and thousands of men died because somebody forgot that the enemy still lived and that the war was NOT over.

Similarly, Satan has been utterly defeated. What appeared to be Satan's greatest victory was actually his ultimate defeat. Christ disarmed Satan and his demonic forces; the enemy was totally humiliated as Jesus triumphed over them at the cross." – *Unknown (sermoncentral.com/ill)*

Today I ask you to consider: have your battles truly ceased? You and I are able to have victory because of the death of Jesus. Many are still looking for their personal victory.

Prayer: Hear me O Lord when I call upon Your Name

Answer my every prayer according to Your Plan

Valid is Your Love that remains forever the same

Every answer we trust because we know You can.

Help each of us be reminded of the sacrifice You made as we face our personal struggles. Help us put our trust completely in You. Amen.

Battles Have Not C.E.A.S.E.D.

"**Nov. 28:** The CIA identifies Michael Spann as the operative killed in the Mazar-e-Sharif prison uprising. Spann officially becomes the first American combat death in the Afghan war. The Pentagon says the Taliban leadership has lost control of their troops. U.S. forces concentrate their attacks on a deep mountain bunker where they suspect Osama bin Laden may be holed up. The bunker is near a complex in Tora Bora. In a radio address to Taliban forces, Taliban spiritual leader Mullah Mohammad Omar, calls on his fighters to 'Stick to your positions, and fight to the death.'" *September11News.com*

"All scripture is inspired by God and is useful for teaching, for showing people what is wrong in their lives, for correcting faults, and for teaching how to live right." *II Timothy 3:16 (NCV)*

Sometimes, no news was the best news. We questioned, we wondered, we hesitated to speak, we searched all in the name of truth. Many a service member still wonders what was true: "I have heard so many different stories. Is this what really happened?"

During the difficulties of heart and soul searching periods, some service members would approach me with simple questions that dealt with what the scriptures have to say and how they applied to what they were dealing with at that time in life. Childhood and parental teaching influenced what they were thinking, and it was my roll to help them recognize the value of seeking the truth offered in Scriptures.

"A single battle can determine the outcome of an entire war. Like Gettysburg and the Invasion at Normandy, a telling battle of the future of England had [come]. General Wellington of the British Army represented the last formidable opposition to the French army under the command of Napoleon. To communicate the outcome of the battle, English towns from Belgium across the English Channel devised a system of flashing lights to be omitted from one church top to another. When the battle ended, England had proved victorious and the message was sent 'Wellington Defeated Napoleon.' As the message was received and sent by each church towards the island of Great Britain, the fog began to rise. By the time the message reached the island, the fog cut the message short as the church received the message 'Wellington Defeated.' For hours, the nation feared the eventual overthrow of their country until the fog lifted and they had the complete message. 'Wellington Defeated Napoleon.' Let us not live believing in an incomplete message." *(Sermon Central Illustration)*

The word "ceased" has the connotation of stopping. Battles having ceased is the hope of all involved, during active battles and during the cleanup following terrorist attacks, but there remains undeniable, underlining and indescribable fears.

- Choices we all make every day.

- Each affects our life in some way.

- Another decision to make I must,

- So where is the message I can trust.

- Expect to find answers when you look,

- Deeply within God's Divine Holy Book

Prayer: Lord, there are so many people that want the battles to cease and the war to be over, in the world and in their personal lives. Help us start looking for the truth in the only place there is real truth. Let us honor the words from Your Son: "If you hold to my teaching, you are really my disciples. Then you will know the truth, and the truth will set you free." *(John 8:31-32)* Let our prayer be that each might find that truth and be set free, becoming victorious through the love portrayed in Your Holy Words. Amen.

Chapter 9

Undergirding Was Available (57-63)

"Please take care lifting each anxious moment"

"Finally, it is my fervent prayer to that Almighty Being…that He will so overrule all my intentions and actions, and inspire the hearts of my fellow-citizens, that we may be preserved from dangers of all kinds and continue forever a united happy people." *– Andrew Jackson*

P.L.E.A.S.E.

"He leads me in the paths of righteousness [uprightness and right standing with Him – not for my earning it, but] for His name's sake." *Psalm 23:3b AMP*

"**Nov. 29**: The Northern Alliance and a group of exiles loyal to the former king agree to a transitional government to rebuild Afghanistan, until more conclusive talks can be convened in the spring. The Northern Alliance also softened their stance on foreign troops in Afghanistan; saying if the need for help becomes 'inevitable' then the Alliance would not oppose an international force. American warplanes continue to bombard the Taliban's final stronghold in Kandahar. The U.S. bombing is described as some of the most punishing air strikes in the war." *September11News.com*

Abraham's servant prayed: "May it be that when I say to a young woman, 'Please let down your jar that I may have a drink,' and she says, 'Drink, and I'll water your camels too'—let her be the one you have chosen..." *Genesis 24:14 (NIV)*

How many times have you prayed or cried, "please Lord; make it stop, help me through; show me what to do or let me get a good night's sleep"? "Please" is a word that needs to be applied to many areas of our lives. Many similar cries continued at this point from those who considered the war to be unjust and unfair.

However, the word "please" was not overwhelmingly expressed by those involved during search and rescue or the clean-up phase of 9/11. It was not expressed verbally, but it was expressed in most of the automatic acts of kindness, concern and compassion. People, over and over, went the extra mile to show they were more than pleased to assist, pleased to offer a helping hand, a handout, a place to sleep, food to eat. Joyfully, the requests to please help were heard without a word being said.

"At home, you fight evil with acts of goodness. 'You overcome the evil in society by doing something to help somebody." *President George Bush – January 30, 2002*

God desires us to be willing to choose to please without having to be asked. Let us pray:

- Please, Lord, help me learn how to choose.

- Lead me, that I may be Your living shining light.

- Each person has so very much to lose.

- Addressing the victory available through Your might

- Salvation being the first each must choose,

- Eternity being the main goal in sight.

Lord, we pray that our "please" be joined with the word "thanks" for all You have done and are doing daily for each who believe. Amen.

T.A.K.E.

"**Nov. 30**: Israeli Prime Minister Ariel Sharon visits Ground Zero with New York Mayor Giuliani. Sharon said, 'I can assure you that democracies will defeat the terror.' An anti-Taliban force of Pashtun fighters captures a strategic peak near Kandahar's airport without a fight. A Pashtun aid said, 'Soon you will hear we are advancing on Kandahar. When we are ready, we will make our way north slowly, and in a week or 10 days, we will have the city.'" *September11News.com*

Daniel answered and said: "Blessed be the name of God forever and ever, for wisdom and might are His. And He changes the times and the seasons; He removes kings and raises up kings; He gives wisdom to the wise and knowledge to those who have understanding. He reveals deep and secret things; He knows what is in the darkness, and light dwells with Him" *Daniel 2:20-22 NKJV*

"Selfishness is the source of most interpersonal conflict. Someone is taking something from us (materially, emotionally, socially, etc.) that we don't want to give, and we fight to keep or gain our desires." *(Copyright 1999, Walk Thru the Bible)*

The events of 9/11 were a verification that we live in a world of self-centered, self-serving takers, takers who see little value in the many lives, the property, the lifestyles, that they decide to take to bring honor to their way of thinking.

However, we serve a God who prefers that we become a world full of givers. He has promised to take care of us. God keeps His promises. Will you take Him as your personal protector? He loves all of us, including the soldier, the laborer, the merchant, the child, the drug addict, the prostitute, and you and me.

- **T**each us how to live effectively for You

- **A**noint us to continually follow through

- **K**eep us secure within Your holy love

- **E**ntreat us with strong arms from above.

True; the world is full of takers, but occasionally the news reveals some wonderful stories of givers.

On this day the news also reported "At the U.S. Marines forward base in southern Afghanistan, American troops raise a bamboo pole with an American flag and a flag of New York City. The NYC flag was given to the Marines by New York City firefighters to honor the victims of the World Trade Center attack." *September11News.com*

S. I. McMillen, in his book *None of These Diseases,* tells a story of a young woman who wanted to go to college, but her heart sank when she read the question on the application blank that asked, "Are you a leader?" Being both honest and conscientious, she wrote, "No," and returned the application, expecting the worst. To her surprise, she received this letter from the college: "Dear Applicant: A study of the application forms reveals that this year our college will have 1,452 new leaders. We are accepting you because we feel it is imperative that they have at least one follower."

Prayer: Lord, help us this day, not to live merely to take from others. Help us learn how to follow, giving of ourselves, as well as leading when called, knowing that You call us with a specific purpose, which is to follow Your directions, Your Word and become great leaders, humbled by You, honoring You and Your principles in a world filled with takers. Amen.

C.A.R.E. He Does

"**Dec. 1:** Canadian PM Jean Chrétien and over 8,000 Canadians arrived in New York City to show their affection and support for New York. Mayor Rudolph Giuliani proclaimed the day Canada Loves New York Day. Palestinian suicide bombers kill at least 10 Israelis and injure over 170 in a series of blasts in Jerusalem. Israeli PM Sharon says he plans to return home from New York a day earlier due to the terrorist attacks.

Dec. 2: U.S. Attorney General John Ashcroft announced that the Canada-U.S.A. border will be patrolled by the U.S. National Guard, to allow overworked U.S. customs agents to return to regular duties. Another suicide bomber kills at least 15 people and injures over 40 in a powerful bus explosion in the Israeli port city of Haifa. President Bush said, 'This is a moment where the advocates for peace in the Middle East must rise up and fight terror.' The body of Johnny (Mike) Spann, the first known U.S. combat casualty, arrives at Andrews Air Force Base with a Marine honor guard.

Dec 3: U.S. Homeland Security Director Tom Ridge tells Americans to brace for fresh terrorist attacks, and put the nation on a high state of alert. Ridge said, 'We are a nation at war. There are shadowy soldiers. This is a shadowy enemy.'" *September11News.com*

"He found him in a desert land and in the wasteland, a howling wilderness; He encircled him, He instructed him, He kept him as the apple of His eye." *Deuteronomy 32:10 NKJV*

The winter had set itself upon us with cold winds and light blankets of snow. The wash-down points left a constant chill in the air, incessantly nipping at the fingertips. For some of the service members, this was their first time having to serve outside during the winter months. It was truly a physical and emotionally chilling experience for them. The dampness of everything that had to be wet down before departing the area added to it. It was during some of these nights that the normal level of grumbling and complaining increased, with understandable reason.

Therefore, a scripture dealing with being surrounded by God's love in the desert land posed a warming thought.

Words of God's unmatched care are what the people of the city, the laborers, the volunteers and the service members, needed to be reminded of. Knowing God's caring never stopped is what many were looking for but unaware of. What was needed and what was actually received through the kind acts portrayed in individual Christ-like attitudes portrayed those who truly cared. Individuals have an indwelt strong desire and need to provide personal care for someone, anyone. If you and I care that much; think how much God cares.

- **C**ry if your day calls for it,

- **A**llow your feelings to be revealed.

- **R**each to God right where you sit

- **E**njoy His care wherein you're sealed.

Chuck Swindoll said, "God knows, my friend and He does care. Please believe that! He not only knows and cares – He understands, He is touched, He is moved, entering into every pulse of anguish, He longs to sustain and deliver us." (Day by Day, *Charles Swindoll, July 2005, Thomas Nelson, inc., Nashville, Tennessee).*

Scriptures tell us further: "The world is full of so-called prayer warriors who are prayer-ignorant. They're full of formulas and programs and advice, peddling techniques for getting what you want from God. Don't fall for that nonsense. This is your Father you are dealing with, and He knows better than you what you need." *Matthew 6:7-8 MSG*

Charles Spurgeon affirms: "There is One who cares for you. His eye is fixed on you, His heart beats with pity for your woe, and His omnipotent hand shall bring you the needed help. The darkest cloud shall scatter itself in showers of mercy. He, if you are one of His family, will bind up your wounds and heal your broken heart. Do not doubt His grace because of your tribulation, but believe that He loves you as much in seasons of trouble as in times of happiness. If God cares for you, why do you need to care too? Can you trust Him for your soul and not your body? He has never refused to bear your burdens; He has never fainted under their weight. Come, then, soul! Say good-bye to anxiety, and leave all your concerns in the hand of a gracious God." (From a sermon by Ryan Akers *Show Me The Money?* 1/19/2009)

Prayer: Heavenly Father, we thank you for previous holy leaders who gave us simple and yet profound words – "The fact of Jesus' birth is the final and immeasurable proof that God cares." (*William Barclay)* Thank you for Jesus' birth and all the care You have showed this world since that time. Let Your love and care continue to guide us. Amen.

L.I.F.T.I.N.G. As Needed

"**Dec. 4:** The Israeli-Palestinian conflict continues to worsen as Israel brands Yasser Arafat's Palestinian Authority a 'supporter of terrorism.' Israeli warplanes strike at eight Palestinian facilities in the West Bank and Gaza, and Israeli bulldozers destroy the runway at Gaza International Airport. The Bonn delegates broke into applause and handshakes after the deal was announced. Speaking from Kabul, Northern Alliance Foreign Minister Abdullah Abdullah said, 'The transition of war to peace is taking place in a very smooth manner.' *September11News.com*

"I waited patiently for the LORD; he turned to me and heard my cry. He lifted me out of the slimy pit, out of the mud and mire; he set my feet on a rock and gave me a firm place to stand. He put a new song in my mouth, a hymn of praise to our God. Many will see and fear and put their trust in the LORD." *Psalm 40:1-3 (NIV)*

The news reveals how we of the world are good at both tearing down and lifting up. Acts of destruction compete with words of affirmation. The Lord is listening and wants to lift us up, especially in our most downcast hour.

"An old time evangelist passed the hat for an offering, and when it came back, it was embarrassingly empty. He shook the hat to make sure that it was empty, and then lifted his eyes to heaven and said, "I thank thee, Lord, that I got my hat back from this congregation." – Unknown

"A man fell into a pit and couldn't get himself out.

- A subjective person came along and said, "I feel for you down here."
- An objective person walked by and said, "It's logical that someone would fall down there."
- A Pharisee said, "Only bad people fall into pits."
- A mathematician calculated how deep the pit was.
- A news reporter wanted the exclusive story on the pit.

- An IRS agent asked if he was paying taxes on the pit.

- A self-pitying person said, "You haven't seen anything until you've seen my pit."

- A fire-and-brimstone preacher said, "You deserve your pit."

- A Christian scientist observed, "The pit is just in your mind."

- A psychologist noted, "Your mother and father are to blame for your being in that pit."

- A self-esteem therapist said, "Believe in yourself and you can get out of that pit."

- An optimist said, "Things could be worse."

- A pessimist claimed, "Things will get worse."

- "Jesus, seeing the man, took him by the hand and lifted him out of the pit." *(PreachingNow Newsletter, August 6, 2002)*

Prayer: Lord we are grateful for the way You go about lifting us with wholeness: body, soul and spirit. We pray that You would:

- **L**ift us each day with Your presence

- **I**mplore us to walk filled with Your boldness

- **F**ulfill us completely through Your love

- **T**each us the whole truth within Your Word

- **I**nspire us continually by Your essence

- **N**urture us always in Your holiness

- **G**ive us peace from Your support above. Amen.

E.A.C.H. Has A Choice

"**Dec 5:** U.S. President Bush said, 'I, along with the rest of America, grieve for the loss of life in Afghanistan. I want the families to know that they died for a noble and just cause.' The U.N. announces from Bonn that Hamid Karzai, a western-educated Pashtun who is leading 40,000 troops in the assault on Kandahar, will assume control of the provisional Afghan government on December 22nd. Karzai said, 'My priority will be peace and stability.'" *September11News.com*

"You have said, 'It is futile to serve God. What did we gain by carrying out his requirements and going about like mourners before the LORD Almighty?" *Malachi 3:14 (NIV)*

Sometimes people feel that life, for them, is futile and accomplishes little. I pray our service members never feel that way. Every task supports another task, the tasks united together to accomplish a mission that just might save some lives, maybe even their own.

Is it futile to serve God? Not all choices that you or I make are the best. The first couple months while serving in the city I had an enlisted assistant who drove me through the city. This was his home, and he knew the routes so much better than I did. He also knew the places to eat. He is the one who took me to that wonderful restaurant that I spoke of earlier, the restaurant that was open for the workers and service members who supported the victims of 9/11.

One night as we were visiting the outer guard positions, I mentioned to him that I did enjoy sushi once in a while. Therefore, he stopped that night – actually it was early morning – and purchased some veggie sushi wrapped in rice. The take-out tray came with the sushi lined up neatly, along with two sauces on the side. I personally had never paid any attention to the sauces before; I simply ate the sushi. The red sauce looked interesting, but the green sauce looked more like a lump of pudding on a leaf. Not knowing what was what, I took the pudding, later learning this green pudding was called **wasabi.** I rolled the lettuce leaf around the wasabi and put the whole thing in my mouth. When my assistant returned to our vehicle, I was having trouble breathing, and he was starting to panic. I gulped some water and gasped to regain my breath, something that did not happen automatically. Meanwhile my assistant was saying I can't believe it. I have a chaplain who survived Viet Nam and Desert Storm, and now I kill him in New York City with wasabi. His demeanor settled, and relief was seen on his face as I returned to my natural color and composure. However, the bad choice gave me a great sermon illustration about the choices we make.

"An Arab chief tells a story of a spy who was captured and then sentenced to death by a general in the Persian army. This general had the strange custom of giving condemned criminals a choice between the firing squad and the big, black door. As the moment for execution drew near, the spy was brought to the Persian general, who asked the question, "What will it be: the firing squad or the big, black door?"

The spy hesitated for a long time. It was a difficult decision. He chose the firing squad. Moments later shots rang out confirming his execution. The general turned to his aide and said, "They always prefer the known way to the unknown. It is characteristic of people to be afraid of the undefined. Yet, we gave him a choice."

The aide said, "What lies beyond the big door?"

"Freedom," replied the general. "I've known only a few brave enough to take it." *(SermonCentral.com/ill)*

As you live each day, you might want to consider choosing God and find true relief and freedom. Speaking from experience, you would enjoy life much more fully if you allow God to:

- **E**cho – the words of His joy in your soul.

- **A**nnounce – the victory of His love in your lives.

- **C**hallenge – the ways of your purpose in His activities.

- **H**arness – the wrong paths that cause you to stumble.

Prayer: Join me as I pray. Lord, You know me and the choices I have made over the years. You know that not all of my choices have been great. I ask Your forgiveness. I look to You for enablement to grow in the wisdom that comes from You that I may learn to ask before I leap into the choices I make. Let my choices bring glory to You. Amen.

A.N.X.I.O.U.S. Living

"**Dec. 6**: Interim Afghan leader Hamid Karzai announces the surrender of Taliban forces in the southern stronghold of Kandahar. U.S. Secretary of Defense Donald Rumsfeld quickly spoke out against amnesty for Taliban Supreme Leader Mullah Mohammed Omar, saying, 'Would an arrangement with Omar be consistent with what I've said? The answer is no.' If amnesty was granted to Omar, Rumsfeld said 'co-operation and assistance' with opposition forces 'would clearly take a turn south.' Rumsfeld orders an investigation into the friendly fire death of three American Green Beret soldiers who died near Kandahar on December 5th after a B-52 bomber dropped a 900-kilogram bomb near front line U.S. troops. Senior U.S. officials say they are providing air support for Alliance troops fighting the al-Qaeda forces near cave complexes in Tora Bora, south of Jalalabad." *September11News.com*

"Casting the whole of your care [all your anxieties, all your worries, all your concerns, once and for all] on Him, for He cares for you affectionately and cares about you watchfully." *1 Peter 5:7 AMP*

The world outside the city offered so much anxious living, as we read the daily news. Although, it was almost four months after the terrorist attack, there were still moments and events within the city that caused personal feelings of anxiety for others and me.

The faded wall of teddy bears in memory of the missing and identified children would nauseatingly stir my heart, and occasionally my stomach, as I passed by making my rounds on the perimeter. I would experience my anxiety level peek while considering how I would feel if one these children belonged to me. I have witnessed that the loss of a child causes indescribable anxiety, grief and deep sorrow.

The only time I ever saw my father cry was when my older sister died. I will never forget his words: "No child should ever die before their parents." However, the wall of teddy bears created wondrous release for the many who experienced this anxiety, intermixed with strong thoughts and emotions – no way around it.

An unknown author defines one simply method to handle an anxious moment: "A first grader, on her first day of school, went to a newly-integrated school, at the height of the segregation storm. An anxious mother met her at the door to inquire, "How did everything go, honey?"

"Oh, Mother! You know what? A little black girl sat next to me!" In fear and trepidation, the mother expected trauma but tried to ask calmly: "And what happened?" "We were both so scared that we held hands all day."

When we face an anxious moment as a child of God let us:

- Always be ready to do our part,

- Noting a determination to lead.

- EXamine with good intentions from the start

- Ideally doing our best to succeed.

- Openly putting forth our very best

- Understanding this is simply a test.

- Supporting – it is God's part to do the rest.

Children, who live with simple faith, have a tendency to see God's part before we adults do. For example:

"A worried mother wondered where her daughter was on the rainy school day afternoon. She should have been home by now. The rain was heavy, the thunder loud, and the lightning was bright.

Finally, after a few anxious minutes, she decided to put her coat on and look for her late child. Out the door and down the street toward the school she went. As she turned the far corner of their street, she spotted her daughter, walking slowly and smiling largely, toward home. The daughter spotted her mom and ran to her, grinning from ear to ear. 'Where have you been? Don't you know that [there] is lightning, and you could be killed?' said the anxious mother. 'But, Mom,' replied the wide-eyed little girl, 'isn't this neat? The puddles, the rain, the boom-booms; and besides, God is taking my picture!'" *(Sermoncentral. com/ill)*

Prayer: Our anxieties we turn over to You, Lord. Let us trust Your Word: "Therefore, stop worrying about tomorrow, because tomorrow will worry about itself. Each day has enough trouble of its own." *(Matthew 6:34* CEB*)* Let us grow in the strength of Your loving support and heartfelt provision. Amen.

M.O.M.E.N.T. By Moment

"**Dec 7:** Speaking aboard the USS Enterprise docked in Norfolk, Virginia U.S. President George W. Bush says the military is "succeeding" in the liberation of Afghanistan. Bush added, "We are a long way from finishing. Much difficult and dangerous work is to be done." Bush was on the carrier for a ceremony commemorating the 60th anniversary of the Japanese attack on Pearl Harbor. American ships in the Arabian Sea board cargo ships in the area searching for fleeing Al-Qaeda commanders. Israeli F-16 jets destroy PLO leader Yasser Arafat's police headquarters in Gaza City. Mayor Rudolph Giuliani, firefighters, rescue workers, and relief workers hold a ceremony in New York, where a Christmas tree trucked from Canada, is lit near the site of the World Trade Center's Ground Zero." *September11News.com*

"Show us Your great power, LORD. You promised that You love to show mercy and kindness. And You said that You are very patient, but that You will punish everyone guilty of doing wrong – not, only them but their children and grandchildren as well." *Numbers 14:17-18 CEV*

The minutes crawled during the wee hours of the mornings some nights, especially during the extremely cold nights of winter. There were those whose guard post offered little shelter and only a heating barrel to keep warm. One or two service members would keep warm by the barrel, while others stationed at that post would curl up in a sleeping bag or be taken to another place to warm up and be brought back. Either way, those nights tiptoed by delaying personal fulfillment of the desire to get inside and warm up.

We, as a society who live in our fast-paced world – even more so in the inner city, find it difficult to deal with life when things seem so slow. God works that way for a reason. A good illustration of this follows:

"Elmer Towns tells about a member of a motorcycle gang who was dramatically converted to Jesus Christ, and the first Sunday he did the only thing he knew he should do; he went to church. Nobody in the church knew him, and he walked down to the second aisle and sat in the seat. And the people stared because he looked the part of a motorcycle gang member: big, burly, bearded, long hair, black jacket, and tattoos.

Announcement time came, and the minister got up and made an appeal for nursery workers. He said, "We need someone to work in the nursery." But no one would volunteer. He asked a second time: "We really need someone to go be with our kids." But no one would volunteer. And the cyclist prayed, "Lord, I want to do what you want me to do, and if you want me to go work in nursery, just have the preacher ask a third time." And a third time the preacher asked, "Please, we need someone to work in the nursery." And the cyclist raised his hand, nodded his head and started toward the nursery. And immediately, 50 mothers followed, volunteering to work in the nursery."

You may ask: did God provide for the need, or was it because the biker offered to help that the need was met? I am inclined to see situations like these as "God Moments." God calls us to listen and respond to moments of opportunity in our life." *(Sermoncentral.com/ill)*

- **M**oment by moment we are called to live a Holy Life

- **O**penly and honestly reaching out to others needs.

- **M**any times we are challenged by personal strife

- **E**ntangled with a life constantly full of unholy weeds.

- **N**ow is the time to ask for help to achieve a Holy Life

- **T**rust God to help you sow and grow Holy Seeds.

Prayer: Let our individual moments represent You, Lord. It is so easy to stray in our thinking and our actions, and for this, Lord, I join with those around me, once again, to ask Your forgiveness. Create in us a desire to have a life of ongoing moments that develop and grow into a strong love relationship with You, O God. Amen.

Chapter 10

Notable Love Was Available (64-66)

". . . showing great love."

"America seeks no earthly empire built on blood and force. No ambition, no temptation, lures her to thought of foreign dominions. The legions which she sends forth are armed, not with the sword, but with the cross. The higher state to which she seeks the allegiance of all mankind is not of human, but of divine origin. She cherishes no purpose save to merit the favor of Almighty God." – *Calvin Coolidge*

S.H.O.W.I.N.G Great Love

Yes, though I walk through the [deep, sunless] Valley of the **Shadow of Death**, I will fear or dread no evil, for You are with me. *Psalm 23:4a AMP*

"**Dec 8:** "The Washington Post reports that the United States has obtained a videotape of Osama Bin Laden describing the damage to the World Trade Center as being much greater than he had expected. According to senior U.S. government officials, the tape was obtained in Afghanistan during the search of a private home in Jalalabad. In the tape, bin Laden praises Allah for success, and he uses language that indicates he was familiar with the planning of the attacks. Bin Laden explains on the tape how he expected only the top of the World Trade

180

Center to collapse, and bin Laden also indicates that more destruction is coming.

Dec 9: Eighteen Northern Alliance soldiers including several commanders are killed in a helicopter crash in northern Afghanistan. The United Nations begins a massive wheat distribution relief effort in Kabul. The astronauts and cosmonauts aboard the Space Shuttle Endeavor and the International Space Station pay tribute to those who died on Sept. 11 and those who are fighting terrorism. Endeavor is carrying thousands of small flags to be distributed to relatives of the victims. Also sent to space was a U.S. flag that was flying at the World Trade Center on the morning of the attacks.

Dec. 10: Kofi Annan accepts the Nobel Peace Prize in Oslo Norway. Annan said, 'We have entered the third millennium through a gate of fire. If today, after the horror of 11 September, we see the better, and we see further – we will realize that humanity is indivisible.' U.S. Marines move into the capital city of Kabul and secure the grounds of the American embassy more than 12 years after it was abandoned in the wake of the Soviet withdrawal." *September11News.com*

"Love is patient, love is kind. It does not envy, it does not boast, it is not proud. It does not dishonor others, it is not self-seeking, it is not easily angered, it keeps no record of wrongs. Love does not delight in evil but rejoices with the truth. It always protects, always trusts, always hopes, always perseveres. Love never fails." *1 Corinthians 13:4-8a (NIV)*

Those who were serving needed to be reassured, as they sat in their shadow of death, during the cold, dreary never-ending nights of cleanup efforts within the city. God continues showing us His great love in the midst of all the wars and rumors of war.

- **S**how me Your wonderful ways O Lord.

- **H**old me close to Your loving heart.

- **O**pen me with the power of Your sword.

- **W**arn me of any mistakes on my part.

- **I**nspire me through others who study Your Word.

- **N**otice me with each challenging new start.

- **G**ive me the wisdom to serve You O Lord.

Elisabeth Elliot speaking about the "I know it all" attitude in our society stated: "I think that it touches very closely on our pride. We think that we've arrived somehow, somewhere; and the Lord is teaching us that up until the very moment when He calls us home, He is our teacher."

Prayer: Lord, we so much need strong leadership as we look at the troubles within our world. We see death and destruction more often than we see love and affection. Our daily news overpowers those who serve in our military – on the front lines, in the security bunkers, on the shore lines, and in the air – with strong discouragement. We look for places, people and resources to help us cope. We ask You, Lord, help us look in the right place and be willing to allow Your Love to show us the best You have for us. We recognize our own weakness when it comes to showing our love in this world of hate, selfishness, bitterness and distrust. Let us know the sincere, free and generous love that You offer. Let Your Love become prevalent in our lives in order that each day will become one that we can look back at and say thank you, Lord! Amen.

Showing G.R.E.A.T. Love

"**Dec. 11:** U.S. aircraft resume bombing of the last stronghold of Osama bin Laden's al-Qaeda forces after a 'surrender or die' deadline passed without any sign of compliance. Zacarias Moussaoui, the so-called 20th hijacker, becomes the first person charged in connection with the planning of the September 11 attacks. Investigators believe Moussaoui, who was arrested in Minnesota in August, may have been the fifth member of the team of hijackers on Flight 93. The 3-month anniversary of the September 11 attacks is remembered across America at 8:46 A.M. EDT, with services at Ground Zero, the White House, the Pentagon, and near the crash site of Flight 93." *September11News.com*

"Give and you will receive. Your gift will return to you in full – pressed down, shaken together to make room for more, running over, and poured into your lap. The amount you give will determine the amount you get back." *Luke 6:38 NLT*

These special events stirred the feelings, anxieties, frustrations and hopes of all who were still serving to finalize the slow process of clean up and terror protection. Every year across America, as we mark the anniversary of the terrorist attacks of 9/11, the memories of the sacrifices made remind us of the irreplaceable, unmistakable generosity of many. Does this reminder help us ask ourselves how much of our life today encourages others to give of their best?

"The late Danny Thomas lost his life savings of $600.00 at a time when he was out of work. He and his wife, Rosie, had a baby on the way, and they needed money. Danny worked at part-time jobs so Rosie could buy groceries. He also borrowed money from friends. It was a tough time in his life.

A week before the baby was born; Danny had the grand total of seven dollars and eighty-five cents to his name. What would he do? "My despair led me to my first exposure to the powers of faith," Danny would later recall.

On Sunday morning Danny went to church. When the offering plate was passed, he put in his "usual one dollar." But something unexpected happened that day. A special missions offering was taken. The priest explained where the mission offering would go, and Danny felt he had to give something. "I got carried away," Danny said, "and ended up giving my seven dollars."

He had given away all his money that Sunday. What in the world had he done? He walked up to the altar rail, got on his knees and prayed aloud. "Look, I've given my last seven bucks," he prayed. "I need it back tenfold because I've got a kid on the way, and I have to pay the hospital bill." He went home with a mere eighty-five cents in his pocket – all the money he had in the world.

"You won't believe this," Danny Thomas later wrote, "but the next morning the phone rang in the rooming house hall." It was a job offer. He was offered a part in a commercial. The job wasn't much, but the pay was good – seventy-five dollars. "I literally dropped the telephone receiver," Danny remembered. "First I whooped with joy; then an eerie feeling came over me." He remembered what he had prayed at church the day before. "The seventy-five dollar fee," he said, "unheard of for me at that time was almost exactly ten times the amount of money I had donated to the church." Source: *Like Parent, Like Child* by Dr. Arthur G. Ferry, Jr. Illustrations for October 20, 2002

- **G**ive of your best in all that you do

- **R**eally, what else would you expect?

- **E**njoy each experience that is new

- **A**llowing others to accept or reject.

- **T**rust God – your work will prove true.

Prayer: Lord, we are so grateful for all the wonderful memories You bring our way. However, when we look back to 9/11 we are stirred and once again challenged in our walk with the Father, Son and Holy Spirit. Do we ask ourselves: am I offering great gifts of love similar to what was seen there? Remind me when I consider this time of year, and help me reconsider my life and asking myself. How am I offering what You have given me to those around, because of Your love? Amen.

Showing Great L.O.V.E.

"**Dec 12:** All four crew members are rescued from the Indian Ocean after a U.S. Air Force B-1 bomber malfunctions and crashes. U.S. Homeland Security Director Tom Ridge and Canadian Foreign Minister John Manley sign a 30-point 'smart border' action plan in Ottawa. Palestinian gunmen ambush a bus outside the Jewish settlement of Emmanuel, killing ten passengers. Soon after the attack Israel cuts contact with Yasser Arafat, and the Israeli government indicates their military would commence widespread." *September11 News.com*

"But God shows and clearly proves His [own] love for us by the fact that while we were still sinners, Christ (the Messiah, the Anointed One) died for us." *1 Corinthians 13:13 AMP*

- **L**ove is continual and available to one and all.

- **O**pen your arms and receive His majestic call.

- **V**oice joyfully your love to everyone you see.

- **E**njoy the life God has directed for you and me.

"An article in a *National Geographic* magazine provides a penetrating picture of God's love for us. After a forest fire raged through a section of Yellowstone Park, one of the rangers found the charred body of a bird at the base of a smoking tree stump. When he knocked it with a stick, three tiny little birds scurried from under their dead mother's wings. The remains of a half burnt nest nearby told the rest of the story. When the raging flames spread up the tree, the half burnt nest fell to the ground and the mother lit near it so her young birds could find protection under her wings. As the flames flared around her, she gave her life that her babies might live." *Sermoncentral.com/Ill*

Obvious strong and powerful levels of love remained 3 months later. City people who were not directly involved in the clean-up process and were able to return to work have already returned to a semi–regular routine. Others whose schedule would allow remained to provide food, sleep areas, and individual support. Whereas the service members, some with jobs waiting, continued to serve patiently at guard points, airports, shorelines, nuclear centers and places restricted from mention. As Chaplain Conversation about the love of God was a common occurrence. It opened the door for many service members to evaluate their spiritual walk and their understanding about the love of God. Some, still mired in the shadow of death, started to realize the loss they felt in their life without knowing or experiencing the love of God, but were not yet ready to move into God's Holy Light.

Prayer: Lord, today we come before You asking for something that all of us desire, that each of us feels lost without: love. Lord, there are too many who feel love for them does not exist and are searching for someone who truly loves them. Lord, help us to receive and understand the depth of Your Love for us and pass it on. Your Love provides: *Leadership, Opportunity, Victory and Eternal life.* Lord, help us to receive Your extended arms of love with a sincere heart and help those still held in the shadow. Amen.

Chapter 11

I Need To Learn To Listen (67-71)

"Listen, everyone, to God."

An elderly man had serious hearing problems for a number of years. His family tired again and again to convince him to get a hearing aid. Finally, he relented. he went to the doctor and was fitted for a set of hearing aids that allowed him to hear 100 percent.

A month later he went back to the doctor. The doctor said with a smile, "Your hearing is perfect. Your family must be really pleased that you can hear again."

The old man replied, "Oh, I haven't told my family yet. I just sit around and listen to their conversations. I've changed my will three times!" ("Hearing Problems" Crosswalk.com, by Jerry De Luca, Montreal West, Quebec)

L.I.S.T.E.N. For Truth

"Your rod [to protect] and Your staff [to guide], they comfort me." *Psalm 23:4b*

"**Dec 13:** India is put on a full state of alert after gunmen storm India's parliament in a 30-minute shootout that leaves twelve dead. Israeli forces attack positions in Gaza and the West Bank and say Arafat is 'irrelevant.' The Pentagon releases a videotape, found in Jalalabad in November, clearly showing Osama bin Laden's full knowledge of the September 11 attack details. After days of translation the tape is broadcast worldwide." *September11News.com*

"Listen carefully to what you hear! The way you treat others will be the way you will be treated--and even worse. " *Mark 4:24 CEV*

Daily the service members listened to two things: The news of the day, to see if there were any more terrorist attaches anywhere within the U.S.; and their orders for the day, never knowing what their assignment might be, yet knowing it may change before the day is over. It could even change on an hourly basis.

Each service member represents their branch of service by what they do along with what they say individually, deciding whether the truth is what they heard, believing they can trust those in command. However, there were times of counseling when what a service member did was not what they were told to do. Sometimes, they heard the instruction or orders and misinterpreted them. Other times they chose to do something different because another service member stated it would be better if they did differently. Sound familiar?

Two Horses

"Just up the road from my home is a field with two horses in it. From a distance, each looks like every other horse. But if you stop your car or are walking by, you will notice something quite amazing. Looking into the eyes of one horse will disclose that he is blind. His owner has chosen not to have him put down, but has made a good home for him. This alone is amazing.

If nearby and listening, you will hear the sound of a bell. Looking around for the source of the sound, you will see that it comes from the smaller horse in the field. Attached to her halter is a small bell. It lets her blind friend know where she is, so he can follow her.

As you stand and watch these two friends, you'll see how she is always checking on him, and that he will listen for her bell and then slowly walk to where she is, trusting that she will not lead him astray. When she returns to the shelter of the barn each evening, she stops occasionally and looks back, making sure her friend isn't too far behind to hear the bell.

Like the owner of these two horses, God does not throw us away just because we are not perfect or because we have problems or challenges. He watches over us and even brings others into our lives to help us when we are in need.

Sometimes we are the blind horse being guided by the little ringing bell of those who God places in our lives. Other times we are the guide horse, helping others see. Good friends are like this. You don't always see them, but you know they are always there.

Please listen for my bell and I'll listen for yours." – *Unknown (sermoncentral.com/Illustrations)*

Prayer of Response: Lord

- Let each of us: good thoughts receive. (Help us, Lord)

- Inspect new ideas that come along.   (Help us, Lord)

- Search for truths to lift the heart.   (Help us, Lord)

- Truly give thanks as we believe,   (Help us, Lord)

- Enjoy, rejoice, and sing a song.   (Help us, Lord)

- Never surrender – doing our part.   (Help us, Lord) Amen.

E.V.E.R.Y.O.N.E. Responds

"**Dec 14:** Some Arabic news agencies question the authenticity of the video, which brings a strong response from President Bush who said, 'This is bin Laden unedited. It's preposterous for anybody to think that this tape is doctored. That's just a feeble excuse to provide weak support for an incredibly evil man.' The last remaining large piece of the World Trade Center is prepared for removal from Ground Zero, and NYC officials say the piece will be stored and later used as part of a future memorial. U.S. Attorney General John Ashcroft said an interagency task force will review ways to prevent leaks of classified information." *September11News.com*

"All have sinned and come short of the Glory of God." *Romans 3:23 (NIV)*

"The last remaining large piece of the World Trade Center is prepared for removal..." It was an exhausting and exhilarating time because of the many laborious hours that had occurred to arrive at this point. To those securing the borders and area, it was an indication that their time was shortening and they might soon be able to get back to their lives. Everyone was responding with words of hope about the possibility of their lives returning to a form of normality. For some this was true, whereas others were still months away from being able to return home.

• Each person today is offered the Everlasting Word,

• Verifying it is an individual must.

• Eagerly seek it with depth and sincerity.

• Realizing it has been brought from the heart of the Lord,

- **Y**our present hopes and futures for a life that is just.

- **O**ffered with gentle love and true clarity.

- **N**otice to everyone His love is abundant and adored,

- **E**njoy God's everlasting love as the one you can trust.

"A famous Methodist evangelist named Peter Cartwright was known for his uncompromising preaching. However, one day when the President of the United States, Andrew Jackson, "Old rough and ready," came to Cartwright's church, the elders warned the pastor not to offend the President. In those days, the President had great power to influence a denomination for good or bad. Content that their pastor would not say anything to discredit their church, the elders retired to the back of the sanctuary.

When Cartwright got up to speak, the first words out of his mouth were, "I understand that President Andrew Jackson is here this morning. I have been requested to be very guarded in my remarks. Let me say this: 'Andrew Jackson will go to hell if doesn't repent of his sin!'" The entire congregation gasped with shock at Cartwright's boldness. How, could this young preacher dare to offend the tough old general in public, they wondered.

After the service, everyone wondered how the President would respond to Cartwright. When Andrew Jackson met the preacher at the door he looked at him in the eye and said, "Sir, if I had a regiment of men like you, I could conquer the world." When we appreciate the power of the word of God and the Holy Spirit speaking from the lips of people with conviction, we will make eternal differences." (Sermoncentral.com /Illustrations)

Prayer: Lord, involvement is a difficult concept for some of us to accept when it comes to serving others, for some believe it is not their calling. However, help all of us recognize that we need to respond to our own mistakes and ask Your forgiveness. Lord, "we all have sinned and come short of the glory," (Romans 3:23 NIV) and we all need to turn our lives around and become involved in You, in order to share the gift of forgiving mercy and love. In Your holy name we pray. Amen.

T.O. G.O.D. We Turn

"**Dec 15:** The final standing facade of the World Trade Center's Tower One is toppled and removed for storage.

Dec 16: Rumsfeld held a town meeting with U.S. forces saying 'the President of the United States, the commander-in-chief, is determined to let the world know that our country cannot be attacked without consequences, and you are bringing the consequences.'

Dec. 17: After pounding the Tora Bora Mountains for days, U.S. military officials say the trail has gone cold in the hunt for Osama bin Laden. The U.S. embassy is officially re-opened in Kabul with a flag raising ceremony." *September11News.com*

"Investigate my life, O God, find out everything about me; Cross-examine and test me, get a clear picture of what I'm about; See for yourself whether I've done anything wrong – then guide me on the road to eternal life." *Psalm 139:23 – 24 MSG*

Psalm 139 is one of the service members' favorite passages of scripture, reminding them how well God really knows us, how He knows what they are thinking, and despite that, He still loves us.

Mother Theresa tells the story of ministering to an old woman dying from starvation: "One evening we went out, and we picked up four people from the street. And one of them was in a most terrible condition. I told the sisters, 'You take care of the other three; I will take care of the one who looks worst.' So I did for her all that my love could do. I put her in bed, and there was such a beautiful smile on her face. She took hold of my hand as she said two words only: 'Thank you.' Then she died. I could not help but examine my conscience before her. And I asked: 'What would I say if I were in her place?' And my answer was very simple. I would have tried to draw a little attention to myself. I would have said, 'I am hungry, I am dying, I am in pain,' or something. But she gave me much more; she gave me her grateful love. And she died with a smile on her face. That is the way I want to die, regardless of my circumstances – not with whining and whimpering, not with complaining and bitterness of spirit, but with gratitude on my lips. If I am able to do this, it will bring a smile not only to my face, but to the face of God."

Today we come to God knowing our own frailty and recognizing the strength and support He offers.

Prayer: Lord, lead us to rely totally on You this day. Help each of us be able to:

- Turn our conversations to recognize individual needs and concerns.

- Open our minds to find divine guidance within Your Holy Word.

- Guide our steps toward an avenue of spiritual growth and comfort.

- Obligate our choices to voluntarily follow your plan for the day.

- Direct our paths that we may truly desire to do as You say.

We ask all this Heavenly Father, knowing Your personal desire for us to be close. Lord, we are grateful for Your Son's death that opened the door to the treasures of eternal life. Thank you, Lord. Amen.

Chapter 12

Triumph Is Possibilities (72-76)

"Witness special glory and become blessed"

"Jesus has forced open a door that had been locked since the death of the first man. He has met, fought and beaten the King of Death. Everything is different because he has done so." – *C. S. Lewis*

W.I.T.N.E.S.S. In Action

You prepare a table before me in the presence of my enemies. *Psalm 23:5a AMP*

"**Dec 18:** Secretary Donald Rumsfeld tells the NATO alliance, 'We need to face the reality that the attacks of September 11, horrific as they were, may in fact be a dim preview of what is to come if we do not prepare today to defend our people from adversaries with weapons of increasing power and range.' President George W. Bush signs legislation designating September 11 as Patriot Day in honor of those killed in the September 11 attacks. A flag from the wreckage of the WTC, and signed by firemen, police, NYC officials, and victim's families, is raised over the Kandahar airport. A fire at the 100 year-old Cathedral of St. John the Divine is fought by over 200 NYC firemen." *September11News.com*

"Ananias told Paul, 'The God of our fathers has chosen you to know his will and to see the Righteous One and to hear words from His mouth. You will be his witness to all men of what you have seen and heard. And now what are you waiting for? Get up, be baptized and wash your sins away, calling on His name.'" *Acts 22:14-16 (NIV)*

The news continues as various military members in differing locations get to witness these events. However, for many on duty around New York City, life remains the same – boring, routine, and even laborious. The mission is important and all volunteered to serve, but many are stating their frustrations with the tediousness of the job. It has become a job more than an honor.

Discussion of news events helped, followed by news about what was going on at home, as thoughts of Christmas were drawing closer and closer. The special events engendered speculation as some of the service members wondered what it would have been like to see the flag raised over the Kandahar airport. For those Army, Navy, Marine and Air Force personnel, I am sure it brought them a step closer to home in their hearts and offered a gentle – or perhaps a harsh – reminder of why they were there making their task more palatable.

The verse chosen here is one to remind those who believe, that we are to put our W.I.T.N.E.S.S. into action by:

Writing – "…love and faithfulness…write them on the tablet of your heart." *Proverbs 3:3 NIV*

Inviting – others to participate in the "Abundant Life" God offers. *John 10:10 NIV*

Teaching – "…bring them up in the training and instruction of the Lord." *Ephesians 6:4 NIV*

Nurturing – "…encourage one another daily, as long as it is called today, so that none of you may be hardened by sin's deceitfulness." *Hebrews 3:13 NIV*

Expressing – "The only thing that counts is faith expressing itself through love." *Galatians 5:6 NIV*

Supporting – "You do not support the root, but the root supports you." *Romans 11:18 NIV*

Speaking – "…speaking the truth in love, we will in all things grow up into Him who is the Head, that is, Christ." *Ephesians 4:15 NIV*

"Hold yourself responsible for a higher standard than anybody else expects of you." *Henry Ward Beecher*

Prayer: Heavenly Father, You show us so much love; You offer us wonderful security; You provide unfathomable wisdom through Your Word, for which we are truly amazed. Help us to start living as true witnesses of what You have offered to those who have a desire to know and experience more of You. In Your holy name we pray. Amen.

S.P.E.C.I.A.L. Relationship

"**Dec. 19:** Israel agrees to resume talks with Palestinian Authority President Yasser Arafat. Dozens of al-Qaeda fighters, who were captured in Pakistan after fleeing Tora Bora, revolt against their Pakistani guards and escape into the hills. At least six al-Qaeda fighters and six Pakistani police were killed.

New York City officials said the people killed or missing in the World Trade Center attacks has fallen to less than 3,000. New York's Liberty Island opens for the first time since Sept. 11th.

After 99 days the WTC fires are extinguished, and become the longest burning commercial fire in U.S. history." *September11News.com*

"Here it is in a nutshell: Just as one person did it wrong and got us in all this trouble with sin and death, another person did it right and got us out of it. But more than just getting us out of trouble, he got us into life!" *Romans 5:18-19a (MSG)*

Ninety-nine days later and the flames are finally extinguished. For ninety-nine days service members have been standing guard, feeling the heat when the wind would shift their way, carrying with it the stench of burnt flesh and other elements. Personnel were rotated by shifts, with occasional retrievals from the zone, but most were there for the long haul.

Today they live a different life at home with their families, at their jobs, and with their hopes of an ongoing, trouble-free future. Regrettable to say, I know for a fact – not so much from my experiences during the events of 9/11 but from my time in Desert Storm, where I served as a Chaplain, and Viet Nam, where I served as a Chaplain's Assistant - medic – a certain smell in the air, repeated event, or even some sound might take them, temporally, back to their service in the city.

The desire is to forget and move on. The reality is that forgetting does not always happen. When anyone is reminded of what happened, they need to know God's healing love, not only in the realm of His salvation work. "But more than just getting us out of trouble, He got us into life." *(Romans 5:19a MSG)* That is the special relationship offered to all who chose to follow Him. You and I are special:

- Special, each one is before the heavenly throne.

- Persons, who from birth, have been individually chosen.

- Everyone has been given a special personal call.

- Called to help others make a journey to their heavenly home.

- Individual choices need to be made because sin our soul has frozen.

- All of us are suffering from the first act that brought about the fall.

- Life's real purpose has been provided – remember we are not traveling alone.

"Jackie Robinson was the first black person to play major league baseball. Breaking baseball's color barrier, he faced jeering crowds in every stadium. Players would stomp on his feet and kick him.

While playing one day in his home stadium in Brooklyn, he made an error. The fans began to ridicule him. He stood at second base, humiliated, while the fans jeered. Then shortstop, Pee Wee Reese, came over and stood next to him. He put his arm around Jackie Robinson and faced the crowd. The fans grew quiet. Robinson later said that arm around his shoulder saved his career.

We are sometimes like Jackie Robinson, full of shame. Sometimes, like Jackie, our shame is from nothing we've done. Sometimes our shame is from our own sin and guilt. And like Pee Wee Reese, Jesus comes and slips his arm around us, and bears our shame for us." Sermoncentral .com/illustrations

Prayer: Lord, sometimes we need a reminder about how special we are. We know You are special in our lives but forget how special the purposes is that You have for us individually. Help us believe Your Word which tells us: "But you *are* a chosen generation, a royal priesthood, a holy nation, His own special people, that you may proclaim the praises of Him who called you out of darkness into His marvelous light;" (1 Peter 2:9 NKJV). Help us to accept Your holy healing touch as it flows through all areas of our life. Thank you, Lord. Amen.

G.L.O.R.Y. in Song

"**Dec. 20**: British Royal Marine commandos arrive in Kabul in advance of the arrival of a United Nations multinational security force expected to number about 3,000 peacekeeping soldiers. An Iraqi civil engineer who defected in August claims that Sadam Hussein has accelerated work on biological, chemical, and nuclear weapons. The Pentagon says they might dispatch U.S. Marines to the Tora Bora region in the hunt for Osama bin Laden.

The last remaining building at the WTC is taken down." *September 11 News.com*

"Let everything that has breath, Praise the Lord!" *Psalm 150:6 (NIV)*

The days before Christmas are becoming few, as we see many Christmas decorations from the majestic in the city to the austere in the guard shack. The service members' hearts are producing glimmers of light at the thought of a rotating schedule that would allow them to be home close to the Christmas season, with a few actually able to make it on Christmas Day. Those with their own family were given first choice, but all who desired, got some time off for Christmas.

"A tradition that Evelyn Knowles has chosen for posterity is to sing to her babies. The very first time she held each of her newborn grandchildren cheek to cheek and heart to heart, they heard their grandmother softly sing "Jesus loves me this I know, for the Bible tells me so." Why? Because she wanted to be certain that they would never remember a time when they hadn't known Jesus.

Growing up in church, Evelyn learned all the songs in the book. In her family of 10, singing church songs was second-nature. Sitting on the front porch, riding in the car, or doing dishes "assembly line" style, they would more often than not find themselves bursting into song. Hymns meant little more than an excuse to sing as a child, but hymns became how they instructed in adulthood." – *Evelyn Knowles, Peace on Earth Ministries, Joplin, MO.*

Today I chose to celebrate God's Glory by using lines and titles from the songs of the generations that honor the personhood of Christ. They shine forth His glory *(All are lines from a song)*:

- *Great Is The Lord and Greatly To Be Praised.*

- *Love Lifted Me – When Nothing Else Would Help.*

- ***O**pen My Eyes That I Might See, Glimpses Of Truth You Have For Me.*

- ***R**each Out And Touch The Lord, As He Passes By.*

- ***Y**es Jesus Loves Me This I Know – For The Bible Tells Me So.*

"We need to let go of our intellectual idea of worship and realize there is more to worship than a sermon; we have to let go of our evangelistic notion of worship and reckon with the fact that worship is not primarily directed toward the sinners who need to be converted; we must let go of our entertainment expectations and remind ourselves that we are not in church to watch a Christian variety show. We have gathered together in worship to be met by God the Almighty. God, the Creator of the Universe, the One who sustains our lives, our Redeemer and King, is present through proclamation and remembrance. He wants to communicate to us, to penetrate our inner self, to take up residence within us. And as we go through the experience of meeting with him in this mystical moment of public worship, we are to respond. But response is not just singing a hymn, not just saying a creed, not just saying a prayer. Response, from the very beginning of worship to the end, must be a powerful inner experience of actually being in the presence of God. When we sing a hymn or say a confession or prayer, we are not singing or saying words, but expressing a feeling, bringing our souls, truly responding and communicating to the living and active presence of a loving and merciful God." – *Robert Webber. Worship Is a Verb: Eight Principles for Transforming Worship. Hendrickson Publishers, Inc., 1998. pg 114.*

Prayer: Gloriously, I join with many in our world as I look forward to the time that we celebrate the birth of a baby named Jesus. He was a special gift, like so many other children. However, He was so much more, because He came from the throne of God and brought with Him a gift for all of humanity: **SALVATION**. Father, let us recognize Your Special Gift and be willing to be the modern-day gift He desires this coming Christmas. Amen.

B.E.C.O.M.E. A Child Of God

"**Dec 21:** NY firefighters arrive in Kabul on a mission of remembrance and to bring aid to Afghan orphans.

Dec. 22: A passenger on American Airlines Flight 63 bound from Paris to Miami tries to ignite an 'improvised explosive' in his shoes, but flight attendants and passengers subdue him. After a six-hour pursuit of a North Korean fishing boat suspected of spying, a Japanese Coast Guard patrol boat sinks the fleeing vessel after a fierce gun battle ensued between the two crews. Indian and Pakistani troops exchange gun fire along their border in the disputed state of Jammu and Kashmir. Hamid Karzai takes the oath of office as Afghanistan's interim prime minister in a ceremony in the Afghan capital of Kabul. Karzai pledges to 'fulfill my mission to bring peace to Afghanistan.'" *September11 News.com*

For I did not speak of my own accord but, the Father who sent me, commanded me what to say and how to say it. I know that his command leads to eternal life. So whatever I say is just what the Father has told me to say." *John 12:49-50 NIV 1984*

Rotations were in process as service members were striving to spend some of the Christmas season with their families. I was preparing for the Christmas weekend and Christmas Eve services back at my church. The air was filled with sounds and songs of merriment even for those who knew their Christmas would be in a guard shack. The sad thing was that some stated they would have a better meal and time of fellowship with their fellow service members than they would at home. This did prove to be a great time to remind those serving, about the beginning of a new family that started on the day we call Christmas and encourage them to join the family of Christ.

"If your actions inspire others to dream more, learn more, do more and become more, you are a leader." – *John Quincy Adams*

- **Be** the person God's heart truly desires you to be.

- **Echo** His love in the challenging life you lead.

- **Choose** the Good News of God that others may see.

- **O**ffer His love to others struggling and in need.

- **M**ake every opportunity to help others take heed.

- **E**ternities calling because God wants us full of glee.

"There once was a woman who really felt she had nothing to share with or give to God and his people. During the services, she would sit, sing softly to herself, pray to herself, engage in little small-talk afterward. On Sunday the preacher gave a message on Expressions of Gratitude. When she went home, she thought about the message; she decided to call the preacher and tell him how the message moved her, and she wanted to thank him for being her friend. After that conversation, she thought: 'well that song that David sang, how beautiful was his voice.' She decided to call him and tell him how much she appreciated his singing and how much that song meant to her. Later, she thought about the piano player and how beautifully she played; she decided to write her a note thanking her for playing every Sunday. As she was writing that note, she thought about the Sunday School teacher and decided to write her, then the Children's church teacher; on and on the list went on, as she wrote these notes of encouragement. Finally she realized she did have something to give: encouragement. And she would give it totally. She saw this as her talent for God." – *Unknown*

Prayer: Heavenly Father, hurriedly the calendar moves to finalize the year. The Christmas season rapidly approaches, O Lord. May our celebrations be about more than who bought or received the greatest gift? May it be a solemn reminder that You already provided the best possible gift ever given. The gift was the birth of a Savior. A special gift from You. It cost us nothing more than our reaching out to receive it. Help us to joyfully receive Your Special Gift, unwrap it and give You the glory. Amen.

B.L.E.S.S.E.D. Redeemer

"**Dec 23:** Palestinian leader Yasser Arafat says he will defy an Israeli travel ban and go to Bethlehem for midnight mass in the Church of the Nativity. India and Pakistan rush troops to the Kashmir border after four people are killed in gun battles in the Samba sector of Kashmir. *Time* magazine names New York Mayor Rudy Giuliani as Person of the Year in 2001.

Dec. 24: A senior Afghan official said Osama bin Laden was seen in a remote village in Pakistan near the Afghanistan border. Afghan soldiers continue to comb the Tora Bora caves in search of the top al-Qaeda leaders.

Flight 63 shoe-bomb suspect, Richard Reid, made his first court appearance in a Boston court. Yasser Arafat is denied access to Christmas Eve celebrations in Bethlehem. Arafat's trademark black-and-white keffiya headdress was draped on an empty chair in St. Catherine's church in Bethlehem.

Dec. 25: A rare gun battle near the Jordanian border leaves an Israeli soldier and two attackers dead. India and Pakistan moved warplanes, troops, and missiles to their border as the talk of war between the countries intensified. Indian Prime Minister Atal Bihari Vajpayee said, 'We do not want war, but war is being thrust on us, and we will have to face it.'

General Tommy Franks, aboard the carrier USS Theodore Roosevelt, said that U.S. coalition forces will continue to search the Tora Bora caves for Osama bin Laden 'until we satisfy ourselves that he is there and dead.'" *September11News.com*

"Listen to my instruction and be wise; do not disregard it. Blessed are those who listen to me, watching daily at my doors, waiting at my doorway. For those who find me find life and receive favor from the LORD." *Proverbs 8:33-35 (NIV)*

The news really was not what we wanted to hear, because battles raged throughout the world as we settled down to open Christmas gifts, drink eggnog, watch TV, and visit family. Whereas a skeleton crew of service members was sitting at guard post, some inside, others outside, on this Christmas Morning. I, along with others, had returned home, and had completed the additional services of Christmas season. However, I was required to report back to my unit on the 25th to continue service until an undetermined date. In the midst of all the celebration the news made it plain that the struggles within the world continued on, and others had returned to their creator. *I pray they were ready.*

Christmas, for the majority, remains a special time for giving thanks to the one who created us and sent His most precious, wonderful gift wrapped in swaddling clothes and placed in a manger, not a mansion, not on a hilltop palace but in a stable. Did we, do we see how special this blessed redeemer is this Christmas season?

- **Be** ready to receive on this special day,

- **L**ove that has been freely displayed.

- **E**ternity with no additional price to pay.

- **S**o look at what the Word has relayed,

- **S**alvation's plan was born on Christmas day.

- **E**njoyment is ours if we have not strayed,

- **D**etermine – life with God is truly the best way.

Prayer: We come in celebration with family, friends or comrades this day, Father. Sometimes we get so busy in the busy-ness of Christmas that we don't take time to say **THANK YOU** for Your Son. Help us on this special day to offer a tribute that is ongoing. Help us see the walk of Christ and how His walk and work was meant for us and our families. May we truly recognize Christ as our reason to rejoice and sing, "Joy to the World." Amen.

Chapter 13

Experience Is Strength (77-79)

"Then, offer praise for the strength to handle each personal challenge."

"That is the basis of thankfulness – to remember that we got here with the help of God, and that He is the provider of every blessing we have." *– Melvin Newland, Minister, Central Christian Church, Brownsville, TX*

<u>T.H.E.N. What?</u>

"You anoint my head with oil; my [brimming] cup runs over." *Psalm 23:5b*

"**Dec 26:** For the third straight day no bombs were dropped by American warplanes, who continue to fly over Afghanistan. Shoe bomb suspect, Richard Reid, is confirmed as a British citizen born in London, and Reid is said to be linked to Muslim extremists. Airports worldwide put in new security measures to check shoes for explosives." *September 11News. com*

"John sent his disciples to ask him, 'Are you the one who is to come, or should we expect someone else?'" *Matthew 11:2b-3 (NIV)*

"A little boy who lived far out in the country in the late 1800s had reached the age of twelve and had never in all his life seen a circus. You can imagine his excitement, when one day a poster went up at school announcing that on the next Saturday a traveling circus was coming to the nearby town.

He ran home with the glad news and the question, "Daddy, can I go?" Although the family was poor, the father sensed how important this was to the lad. "If you do your Saturday chores ahead of time," he said, "I'll see to it that you have the money to go."'

Come Saturday morning, the chores were done and the little boy stood by the breakfast table, dressed in his Sunday best. His father reached down into the pocket of his overalls and pulled out a dollar bill – the most money the little boy had possessed at one time in all his life. The father cautioned him to be careful and then sent him on his way to town.

The boy was so excited; his feet hardly seemed to touch the ground all the way. As he neared the outskirts of the village, he noticed people lining the streets, and he worked his way through the crowd until he could see what was happening. Lo and behold, it was the approaching spectacle of a circus parade! The parade was the grandest thing this lad had ever seen. Caged animals snarled as they passed, bands beat their rhythms and sounded shining horns, midgets performed acrobatics while flags and ribbons swirled overhead.

Finally, after everything had passed where he was standing, the traditional circus clown, with floppy shoes, baggy pants, and a brightly painted face, brought up the rear. As the clown passed by, the little boy reached into his pocket and took out that precious dollar bill. Handing the money to the clown, the boy turned around and went home. What had happened? The boy thought he had seen the circus when he had only seen the parade! Are you experiencing all that God has for you? The Christian life is a marvelous adventure, an exciting journey.

John was simply the beginning, the introducer, the one who prepared the way. The best was yet to come; however, many then, as today, missed the great event, expecting more and asking what comes next. We live in a world full of expected immediate results. The Israelite's looked for a coming King, not a Savior." – *Unknown (Sermoncentral. com/ill)*

The year 2001 is coming to an end, a year that has and will affect many people throughout this generation, especially all who served in and around New York City. Measures were being taken to reduce the number of forces on duty. The Critical Incident Stress Debriefing (CISD) teams are becoming more occupied since they are doing the outtake briefing for all personnel scheduled to leave. The teams listened to the hurts and concerns of all who desired; confidentiality was and still is maintained. We offered support referrals where needed, plus we made ourselves available as a follow-up source. Then what? Only time will tell, once they have checked out of the unit.

The scriptures offer some guidelines to answer some of the "then what" questions. God's Word shows many times the evidence in Jesus' words produced the result known as "immediately." Many are still seeing the then time frame and missing the now.

- **T**ake time to be holy – "Now is the Day of Salvation" *2 Corinthians. 2:6 NIV*

- **H**ope in God's presence – "If I could touch the hem of his garment" *Matthew 9:20-22 NIV*

- **E**xpect unbelievable response – "Ask and you shall receive" *Matthew 7:7-8 NIV*

- **N**otice the promises of God – "I am with you always." *Matthew 28:20 NIV*

God's love is not only for **T.H.E.N.**, of the past, it is also **T**errific **H**elp **E**xperienced **N**ow. Praise the Lord!

Prayer: Lord, today we ask You to help us move beyond the past into the present. Help us do more than see the passing parade but identify the present glory. Show us Your Awesome Glory alive and well today, in the churches, streets, cities, homes and throughout the world. Help us to be more than observers but partakers of the beauty of then that is now and available throughout the rest of our lives. Amen.

O.F.F.E.R. Something

"**Dec. 28**: Pakistan and India move closer to all-out war as border troops shell each other in the disputed Jammu-Kashmir region. The Indian army also ordered the evacuation of border towns. Pakistan warns the U.S. they may no longer provide logistic support in the search for al-Qaeda leaders, saying the Pakistani troops are required for support in the looming conflict with India. General Tommy Franks meets with U.S. President Bush at Bush's Crawford, Texas, ranch where Bush tells reporters, Osama bin Laden 'is a guy who three months ago was in control of a country. Now he's maybe in control of a cave. He's on the run.'" *September11News.com*

"So here's what I want you to do, God helping you: Take your everyday, ordinary life – your sleeping, eating, going-to-work, and walking-around life – and place it before God as an offering. Embracing what God does for you is the best thing you can do for Him. Don't become so well-adjusted to your culture that you fit into it without even thinking. Instead, fix your attention on God. You'll be changed from the inside out. Readily recognize what He wants from you, and quickly respond to it. Unlike the culture around you, always dragging you down to its level of immaturity, God brings the best out of you, develops well-formed maturity in you." *Romans 12:1-2 (MSG)*

"Offer" became a word with a new meaning for all the military who served on Christmas Day. The hotels came together in agreement and gave each service member a free night with their families, in a hotel in the area of Times Square. Talk about a new sense of appreciation. Many took advantage of this, including myself. My wife and oldest daughter joined me for a day and night in a hotel that I could never consider the cost of or the magnificence of. I had to work that day, but my wife and daughter enjoyed shopping and looking at the sights together. I did join them for supper. I had no idea that a small slice of cheese cake could cost $7.00. Expense aside, it was an adventure that painted a new picture on the minds of many service people about those who live within New York City. There were no strings attached.

God has presented a similar request in Romans 12:1 to those who believe. This offer is one that you and I get to make. It is a personal choice and a part of our spiritual service. God offered His son, in order that we might have an abundant life. Are you and I truly willing to offer ourselves for Him?

- **O**ne who serves makes an overwhelming choice,

- **F**acing unknown dangers on a daily – even hourly basis.

- **F**ear being a word often spoken in a soft undertone voice,

- **E**veryone realizing there is little chance of an oasis.

- **R**ecognize hope and strength from God is His offer – our choice.

Prayer: Heavenly Father, we are so grateful for the wonderful gift You offered us at Christmas time and how Your Son was willing to offer Himself that we, who are members of this human race, might be able to offer ourselves back to You. Thank you for all blessings that You offer and help us accept, adapt and adore what is right before us in Your hands. Amen.

P.R.A.I.S.E. Is Offered

"**Dec. 29**: American bombers attack a suspected Taliban leadership compound near Gardez, south of Kabul. U.S. defense officials say there are 125 Taliban and al-Qaeda prisoners at a detention facility near Kandahar. The Persian Gulf island nation of Bahrain pledges its best warship to the coalition against terrorism. A senior Afghan intelligence chief claims to have received 'reliable information' that Osama bin Laden paid a 'large amount' of money to an Afghan commander to be taken across the border to Pakistan. U.S. officials are reportedly offering cash 'incentives' to Afghan militia commanders to assist in the hunt for bin Laden." *September 11 News.com*

"'I saw the Lord always before me. Because he is at my right hand, I will not be shaken. Therefore my heart is glad and my tongue rejoices; my body also will rest in hope." *Acts 2:25-26 (NIV)*

"One Thanksgiving season a family was seated around their table, looking at the annual holiday bird. From the oldest to the youngest, they were to express their praise. When they came to the 5-year-old in the family, he began by looking at the turkey and expressing his thanks to the turkey, saying although he had not tasted it, he knew it would be good. After that rather novel expression of thanksgiving, he began with a more predictable line of credits, thanking his mother for cooking the turkey and his father for buying the turkey. But then he went beyond that. He joined together a whole hidden multitude of benefactors, linking them with cause and effect.

He said, "I thank the checker at the grocery store who checked out the turkey. I thank the grocery store people who put it on the shelf. I thank the farmer who made it fat. I thank the man who made the feed. I thank those who brought the turkey to the store."

Using his investigating process, he traced the turkey all the way from its origin to his plate. And then at the end he solemnly said "Did I leave anybody out?"

His 2-year-older brother, embarrassed by all those proceedings, said, "God."

Solemnly and without being flustered at all, the 5-year-old said, "I was about to get to him."

Well, isn't that the question about which we ought to think…?"
– *Getting Around to God, Citation: Joel Gregory, "The Unlikely Thanker," Preaching Today, Tape No. 110*

Thanksgiving is over; Christmas is over. As a result, do we stop giving thanks? The service members were thankful for their night in the hotel; they were thankful that they were not serving outside the country right now; they were thankful that there was a good chance they would celebrate New Year's around their own hometown, possibly having the chance to see the ball drop at Times Square on New Year's Eve. As 2001 was drawing to a close, many, without reservation, discussed areas of thankfulness which they could give praise.

God desires our praises. We are able to offer honest praise by:

- **P**raising the Lord for His birth.

- **R**eaching out and taking His hand,

- **A**ccepting His Holy Love for you.

- Inspiring to live His heaven on earth.

- Serving Him freely in our troubled land.

- Enjoying His blessings – sincere and true.

Prayer: Praise Your name, Heavenly Father, for the many blessings You provided last year, the many blessings You have planned this coming year, as well as the many challenges. I know You have something special in mind for my life. I praise You for the many loves and losses, accomplishments and defeats, struggles and victories. Help me look back, as last year is about to close, and offer to You a word of praise for each day of life You have granted. Amen.

<u>F.O.R. T.H.E. Best</u>

"**Dec. 30**: The chairman of the Senate Intelligence Committee says that Osama bin Laden has likely survived the American military campaign and may have escaped to Pakistan.

An observation platform with an unobstructed view of the World Trade Center's Ground Zero opens with long line-ups in New York City." *September 11News.com*

"…I have learned how to be content with whatever I have. I know how to live on almost nothing or with everything. I have learned the secret of living in every situation, whether it is with a full stomach or empty, with plenty or little." *Philippians 4:11b – 12 NLT*

It was a thrill being on duty in New York City the night the observation platform was opened. I had the privilege of being one of the first to walk up and take a look at the area known as Ground Zero from a perspective different than that which I had seen for the last few months, where I walked at ground level seeing only what was in front of me. Now, for the first time I could look down and see how much was below the ground that I never had seen. I had heard various descriptions from service members who had lived, worked, shopped and visited the Twin Towers before their destruction. But this was different.

I had worked in contentment with the job I was doing, providing the ministry that was necessary. I had my times of "living in every situation" for sleeping and eating. I knew the times of a full stomach – actually that was still one of the easiest things to accomplish. I digress. When I looked in that hole in the ground and saw the former life under it, I recognized that these people who had plenty now had little. How would they move forward?

The answer for those who place their trust in God is simple, because we have learned not to rely only on what we see or can do, what we have accomplished or what is available in our world. We rely on much more.

We have learned to rely upon the resources of God, and they are plentiful.

- **F**ind the joy and peace that is offered by our Lord.

- **O**pen your hearts to the treasures found within His Word.

- **R**each out to comfort one another in time of need.

- **T**rust God's Word to provide a nourishing solid feed.

- **H**ope in the fact God is with every sister and brother.

- **E**xperience His love as you offer it to one another.

Bob Russell writes: "Have you had a taste of the best this world has to offer? You went to Hawaii once on vacation, so now it's harder for you to enjoy the state park. You've eaten a steak at Ruth Chris, so it's harder to be thankful for a meal at Ponderosa. You've driven a Jaguar, so now you can't be as content with your used Chevrolet. You've cheered for a national champion, so now it's difficult to be grateful when your team has a good season but doesn't take home the title."

"Generally speaking, the more we have, the less grateful we are. It should be the opposite; the more we have, the more thankful we should be. But it usually doesn't work that way, does it?"

"A wise man prayed, 'Give me neither poverty nor riches, but give me only my daily bread. Otherwise, I may have too much and disown you and say, 'Who is the Lord?' Or I may become poor and steal, and so dishonor the name of my God'" (*Proverbs 30:8-9). NIV*

"It is a rare person who, when his cup frequently runs over, can give thanks to God instead of complaining about the limited size of his mug!" – *"Jesus, Lord of Your Personality" by Bob Russell, Howard Publishing Co., 2002, pp. 14-16*

Prayer: Lord, as we stop and take a new look down the holes in our life, noticing parts in our life that need to be cleaned up and some that need to be rebuilt. Help us to establish a reconstructed foundation. Help us be part of the foundation to encourage, strengthen, and support each other, enabling ourselves and others to find the best that God has to offer. Let us recognize we can only accomplish this through Your Love for us, in us and through us. Help us to truly be there for the others within our command, our personal life and our sphere of influence in order that we all may grow to glorify You. Amen.

S.T.R.E.N.G.T.H. TO SURVIVE

"**Dec 31:** Michael Bloomberg is sworn in as the new Mayor of New York City taking effect at midnight. Rudy Giuliani closes the NYSE and celebrates New Years Eve with New Yorkers in Time Square.

Jan 1: FDNY Fireman Bill Spade at the Rose Bowl Parade Pasadena, Calif. There was an American Flag Ceremony at the Houses of Parliament in London, UK. Mayor Bloomberg Gives His Inaugural Address in New York City. Taliban Prisoner is escorted from a Kabul Jail. British Marines patrol streets in Kabul, Afghanistan.

Jan 2: FDNY Fireman Reads Messages on NYC Memorial Near Ground Zero. *September11News.com*

Asbestos in dust near Ground Zero feared harmful once airborne; twenty-five percent of firefighters who worked rescue have been ill with respiratory problems...." *(The Morning News)*

"I pray that the eyes of your heart may be enlightened, in order that you may know the hope to which he has called you, the riches of his glorious inheritance in his holy people, and his incomparably great power for us who believe. That power is the same as the mighty strength he exerted when he raised Christ from the dead and seated him at his right hand in the heavenly realms." *Ephesians 1:18-20 (NIV)*

A New Year arrives bringing a new sense of hope. Those who were with me welcomed the beginning of what might hopefully be the end for us and our time of service, knowing that the cleanup would continue for an extended period of time. We all were kind of anxious to return to civilian life; however, very few were complaining about doing their share of federal service simply because they knew it could be considerably worse.

My work was involving more and more Critical Incident Stress Debriefings (CISD) work, as I joined a team and traveled from point to point, which differed from the continual guard stations of the past. I was meeting new people, who were ready to return to their personal life. Some had memories and fears they wanted to have removed, or at least be relieved from, before their journey home. I did my best to direct those with inner struggles to find a new form of strength from the Lord. How well do you know that strength that comes from God?

- **S**urvival is available to all who in Christ believe.

- **T**riumphant life is strengthened for those who receive.

- **R**eal victory is identified when the enemy tries to deceive.

- **E**njoy the strength offered through our personal Savior.

- **N**othing but mercy and forgiveness are given in our favor.

- **G**reatness in God can become our individual flavor.

- **T**rust Him now for His inner strength to survive.

- **H**onor His choice as your walk becomes more alive.

Prayer: As Paul prayed for the church at Ephesus, "I ask—ask the God of our Master, Jesus Christ, the God of glory—to make you intelligent and discerning in knowing Him personally, your eyes focused and clear, so that you can see exactly what it is He is calling you to do, grasp the immensity of this glorious way of life He has for his followers, oh, the utter extravagance of His work in us who trust Him—endless energy, boundless strength! Amen. *Ephesians 1:18-20 MSG*

T.O. H.A.N.D.L.E. Life

"**Jan 7:** Signed Ground Zero Flag Aboard the USS Theodore Roosevelt.

Jan 9: Faces of Ground Zero Exhibit Grand Central Station. The Department of Justice has opened a major criminal investigation into Enron Corp., the once mighty energy trader that filed the largest bankruptcy in United States history." *CNN Money*

This is the day; the one day, I got really upset. I went to see the *Faces of Ground Zero*.

An artist had created a statue and art display of the heroes of 9/11. It was presented in good taste, glowing words with solid, positive presentation of rescuers, medical professionals, food and support effort personnel and other professionals. However, I found not one mention of the military support effort. They apparently, it seemed, went unseen. If they were represented, I did not see them.

Service members served beginning September 11, 2001 and for many months afterward. I personally served 180 days. Admittedly, the military service members were often in the background as support and security. This was a good thing – actually very much like how God takes care of you and me. We know He is there, often in the background, not visible to all.

"The truth of the matter is that you always know the right thing to do. The hard part is doing it." – *General Norman Schwarzkopf*

"I can do all this through him who gives me strength." *Philippians 4:13 (NIV)*

The security and clean up continued in the city, while life moved on for the rest of the world. Fragmentary information in the news on January 8, 2002, informed the world about the firefight that caused the first U.S. death by enemy fire in the war on terror. Sadly, over my 40 years of military life, I have seen too many serious injuries and deaths; I have made several family notifications and conducted many honorable military funerals. Personally, I learned a long time ago I could not handle this type of life by myself. But with God's help providing backup security and strength for me through the Holy Spirit; I learned to handle life and its many issues. So I tell you:

- **Think** about it! – He gives me strength!

- **Only** this strength is much more than physical.

- **How** do I do it? The world is so large.

- **And** filled with so many "should" and "ought's."

- **Needless** to say, who will listen?

- **Direct** me to those who know something is missing.

- **Let** me see Your Divine Plan for me.

- **Encourage** me your servant to be.

Winston Churchill said: "We do not war primarily with races as such. Tyranny is our foe, whatever trappings or disguise it wears, whatever language it speaks, be it external or internal; we must forever be on our guard, ever mobilized, ever vigilant, always ready to spring at its throat. In all this, we march together. Not only do we march and strive shoulder to shoulder at this moment under the fire of the enemy on the fields of war or in the air, but also in those realms of thought which are consecrated to the rights and the dignity of man. Let us rise to the full level of our duty and of our opportunity, and let us thank God for the spiritual rewards. He has granted for all forms of valiant and faithful service." – *Winston Churchill, Monday, 6 September 1943*

Prayer: Life is a gift from You, O Lord, for which we are grateful. Let us recognize that we do not need to handle it all alone, even though we may feel others do not even identify our existence. You are there for us, and sometimes we simply need to be reminded. God, You are great, and great is Your love. Thank you, Lord. Amen.

E.A.C.H. Person Is Important

"**Jan 4**: The deposed Taliban leader Mullah Mohammed Omar may have been arrested, an Afghan minister claimed in the early hours of today. The Afghan minister for reconstruction, Amin Farhang, told German ARD TV news: 'I have heard that he was arrested but more I do not know.' The Taliban's spiritual leader was earlier reported to have been surrounded in his mountain hideout. Talks with those believed to be harboring the cleric were galvanized by threats of US bombing." *The Guardian*

"But if He remains silent, who can condemn him? If He hides his face, who can see him? Yet He is over individual and nation alike." *Job 34:29 (NIV)*

The New Year began with the same questions I face at the beginning of every year. Where do I fit into Your Plan for the year ahead of me? There are those who do not really look forward to starting over. This is expressly true in the church, in the world, and for those who serve within the military. Some people need to be reminded just how important they are, especially to God, as they face new beginnings, even when He remains silent. "He knows what we need even before we ask." (Matthew 6:8 NIV).

- Each and every one of us is known as special in God's sight.

- Announce to everyone the love that you personally know.

- Chances are not everyone may have seen God's special light.

- Help others receive God's individual peace and inner glow.

Sometimes during service to our country, we have times of loneliness and separation, and we wonder if God truly does care or does have a plan for us. Sometimes, He seem so silent; He seems to hide His face, and yet God passionately cares for you and me, as well as the nation we have chosen to serve.

Chuck Swindoll tells us, "During the waiting period, trust God without panic. Count on Him to handle the cupbearers of your life, the people who forget you, the people who break their promises. It's God's job to deal with the cupbearers of your past. It's your job to be the kind of servant He has designed you to be. Be faithful during the waiting periods of life. God will not forget you or forsake you." – *Day by Day, Charles Swindoll, July 2005, Thomas Nelson, inc., Nashville, Tennessee.*

Prayer: Lord, some of the waiting periods seem so long, even unbearable. I try to reason and understand, and I do not succeed. I think there is something I need to do but there isn't. You know what is best for me; lead me not to rely on my own understanding, and show me how to value Your Guidance and realize, without reservation, how special each one of us remains in Your sight. Amen.

P.E.R.S.O.N.A.L. Needs

Jan 11: "Green Berets Honor Guard at Nathan Chapman Funeral.... Four Months After the WTC Attack Firemen Recover More Victims." *September11News.com*

When we gathered for worship, occasionally in the chapel, or often wherever we could; we sang choruses because they were easy to remember. Many times we sang: "It's me, It's me, Oh Lord, standing in the need of prayer." And it truly was! You and I need to recognize that. The Lord who is our Shepherd is personally interested in an ongoing individual relationship with us. How personal is your relationship with God?

- **P**utting God first is a necessary must.

- **E**xperiencing Heaven on earth is a goal.

- **R**eceiving daily instruction and guidance we can trust.

- **S**eeking to make ourselves completely whole.

- **O**perating with the desire to do what is truly just.

- **N**oting, with humble heart, that God has a Divine Role.

- **A**ccepting His leadership to win over all personal lust.

- **L**iving to honor God within our individual personal soul.

"A teenage boy was seriously injured an automobile accident. The doctors did all they could to repair the damages to the boy's body, but despite their fast medical knowledge, they were unable to completely restore his legs. He was informed that he would eventually walk, but only with the aid of braces and crutches. The young man was devastated. His whole life had revolved around sports, with the likelihood of receiving an athletic scholarship in football. He would never run again. He was not even sure that he wanted to walk.

The next year was not easy one for the boy or his parents. Major decisions had to be made, routines established, and attitudes adjusted. Time, prayers, and patience helped to restore some of the boy's confidence in himself, but he still battled daily with lapses into self-pity. One evening the boy's father approached him and said, "get dressed, I want us to go to church tonight and hear the guest preacher." At first the boy protested, but eventually agreed at the father's insistence.

At the conclusion of the sermon, the preacher gave an altar call. The father told his son, "I think we ought to go." The braces thumped loudly on the floor as they went down the aisle. Father and son knelt down to pray, and then returned to the pew. "Thump, thump, thump." Turning to his father, the boy said, "It's okay now, Dad. I still have the braces on my legs, but God has removed them from my mind." Remember, healing happens in many ways." *Sermoncentral.com/ill*

Prayer: Lord, help each of us learn to live with our personal God who endearingly loves us, with unending love, with ever-present love, and with individual love. Help us recognize that You can and will lead us through our personal Shadows of Darkness. Thank you for all the Love you have given over the years and the overwhelming, never-ending love that is unfailing. Amen.

C.H.A.L.L.E.N.G.E. Remains

Jan 12: *John Hendren | Times staff writer – Washington*: "The first clutch of 20 prisoners arrived Friday at a makeshift prison at Guantanamo Bay Naval Base in Cuba, four months after the Sept. 11 attacks that touched off the U.S. war on terrorism and 27 hours after

leaving a Kandahar, Afghanistan prison." [. . .] *Richard C. Paddock |
Times staff writer" – Jakarta, Indonesia:* " A terrorist network broken
up in Singapore last month was closely linked to Al Qaeda and had
planned to attack U.S. military and business targets in the island state,
Singapore's government said Friday. Times Wire Reports – India's
army chief issued a blunt warning to Pakistan, pledging massive
retaliation if it launches a nuclear attack." [. . .] *Mark Casanova* – Lots
of folks lost sleep after Sept. 11. The attacks knocked the equilibrium
right out from under us. But look at it this way: If you lost sleep, you
probably at least had the luxury of a bed to sleep in." *Los Angeles
Times*

"One of the high priest's servants, a relative of the man whose ear Peter
had cut off, challenged him, 'Didn't I see you with him in the garden?'"
John 18:26 (NIV)

Life is and always has been a challenge, regardless of our station in life.
Imagine being in Peter's place when asked "Didn't I see you with Him
in the garden?" Personally, I would have hesitation, fear, and a degree
of uncertainty about what to say or do next. Would I maintain totally
pure morality and up front face the truth? I am not sure! I would hope
so but I am not sure. Even though ready to meet my maker, I am in no
hurry! Moral choices were made in the City and for some that is part of
their shadow that they face; asking did I make the right choice. "I got
out should I have tried to help others?"

An unknown author wrote:

"A man who had regularly prayed for many years began to wonder if God heard his prayers at all. During one of his routine times of prayer, he started this doubting pattern once again. He stopped praying and thought for a moment.

"Enough of this," he said.

He then lifted his eyes toward heaven and yelled, "Hey up there, can you hear me?" There was no response.

He continued, "Hey, God, if you can really hear me, tell me what you want me to do with my life."

A voice from above thundered a reply, "I WANT YOU TO HELP THE NEEDY, AND GIVE YOUR LIFE FOR THE CAUSE OF PEACE!"

Faced with more of a challenge than the man really wanted, he answered, "Actually, God, I was just checking to see if you were there."

The voice from above now answered with disappointment: "THAT'S ALRIGHT; I WAS ONLY CHECKING TO SEE IF YOU WERE THERE." *Sermoncentral.com/ill*

When the challenge comes before us as service members, we usually do not have much of a choice but to meet it head on and do our best to accomplish whatever the challenge may be. In daily life, be it military or civilian, how do you face the challenge? Here are some ideas to consider:

- Choose to love your neighbor – even those difficult to love.

- Help those whom you recognize as having a personal need.

- Answer questions from those searching for hope from above.

- Live giving from within because that is what many need.

- Lead with compassion and sincerity by offering a gentle Godly embrace.

- Encourage the challenged, developing new ways to show heavenly care.

- Nurture love toward others, and help them recognize God's powerful grace.

- Give the Holy Word daily with positive and proven directions to share.

- Entice those around you to seek God's Holy and Loving Face.

This challenge can be met as you and I constantly remind ourselves that we are not alone. Even at the times when we fear for our life, see only the shadows or have to make those tough decisions. The Great Commission that Jesus gave to the disciples applies to us. He gave it to them because He knew the challenges and the choices that were ahead. He knows us also and the same words apply: "I am with you always, *even* to the end of the age." *Matthew 28:20 (NKJV).* He is there with outstretched arms even when we make a bad choice.

Prayer: Heavenly Father, we thank you for Your Love and the Son who faced His life destroying challenges. We thank you that He came so that we could enjoy a full life through the power of Your Holy Spirit. Forgive us our bad choices, our moral dilemmas, and our lack of faith. Help each of us first recognize any challenge You place before us. Then help us rely upon You, Your Word and those You place in our lives, that we may be victorious and glorify You in all that we do. Thank you for trusting us enough to challenge us. Amen.

Chapter 14

Delight Is In Others (80-86)

". . . and help us encourage and strengthen one another."

"All the blessings we enjoy are Divine deposits, committed to our trust on this condition, that they should be dispensed for the benefit of our neighbors." – *John Calvin*

H.E.L.P. U.S. Celebrate

"Surely or only goodness, mercy, and unfailing love shall follow me all the days of my life, and through the length of my days." *Psalm 23:6a AMP*

Jan 14: "U.S. Soldiers Find Arms Cache in Afghan Caves Near Zhawar Kili South East of Kabul." (*September11News.com*). "Bush Administration to Roll Back Key Provisions of 1972 Clean Air Act." *www.ironictimes.com* BBC News: US President George W Bush said he felt "great" on Monday, despite having fainted and fallen from a couch after choking on a pretzel over the weekend." *news.bbc.co.uk*

"Hear my cry for mercy as I call to you for help, as I lift up my hands toward your Most Holy Place." *Psalm 28:2 NIV*

The New Year is now well under way. Have you set new goals and objectives for the year and broken them already? Have you asked your Lord and Savior to be your personal guide for this year? Have you asked God's help before a time of crisis arises? Have you asked your Lord to help you walk through your shadows and valleys?

"The researchers say that while these studies are, in certain respects, the sort of work that invariably follows major disasters and accidents, they also say that the variety of the inquiries reflects a disturbing but ever-growing realization among health experts: four months after the attacks, very little can be said with scientific certainty about the health risks that recovery workers or bystanders faced in the disaster and the cleanup.

That uncertainty, which some health and environmental experts now say was perhaps not adequately reflected by public officials in the days and weeks after the attacks, underscores how unique the World Trade Center disaster was as a public health emergency.

The blast of dust and smoke -- and the toxic substances, fibers and ash that blew through New York in the days afterward -- is without precedent in medical literature, which means that there are no studies to fall back on for guidance on whether to be alarmed or reassured." *By KIRK JOHNSON Published: January 11, 2002 NY Times*

- How often, Lord, we call out during times of distress.

- Enrich us daily with Your Holy Blessings.

- Lead us to Your Everlasting Strength anew.

- Place within us a peace that is not guessing.

- U provide each and every blessing

- Strengthen us with Your Word which is true.

  - "We wait in hope for the LORD; he is our help and our shield." *Psalm 33:20 NIV*

  - "But as for me, I am poor and needy; may the Lord think of me. You are my help and my deliverer; you are my God, do not delay." *Psalm 40:17 NIV*

  - "God is our refuge and strength, an ever-present help in trouble." *Psalm 46:1 NIV*

  - "Surely God is my help; the Lord is the one who sustains me." *Psalm 54:5 NIV*

  - "Because you are my help, I sing in the shadow of your wings." *Psalm 63:7 NIV*

  - "The LORD is with me; he is my helper. I look in triumph on my enemies." *Psalm 118:7 NIV*

- "My help comes from the LORD, the Maker of heaven and earth." *Psalm 121:2 NIV*

- "Blessed are those whose help is the God of Jacob, whose hope is in the LORD their God." *Psalm 146:5 NIV*

- "For I am the LORD your God who takes hold of your right hand and says to you, Do not fear; I will help you." *Isaiah 41:13 NIV*

- "He said: 'In my distress I called to the LORD, and he answered me. From deep in the realm of the dead I called for help, and you listened to my cry.'" *Jonah 2:2 NIV*

- "Let us then approach God's throne of grace with confidence, so that we may receive mercy and find grace to help us in our time of need." *Hebrews 4:16 NIV*

- "So we say with confidence, 'The Lord is my helper; I will not be afraid. What can mere mortals do to me?'" *Hebrews 13:6 NIV*

Prayer: Lord H.E.L.P. U.S. this day to take Your Holy Words and apply them directly to our daily existence, including all whom we come in contact with. Let Your Words be the cornerstone of our foundation, that we might lift others up out of their shadows to the solid ground. For this we give You thanks. Amen.

E.N.C.O.U.R.A.G.E. One Another

"**Jan 18:** ISLAMABAD, Pakistan (CNN) – "Pakistan's president says he thinks Osama bin Laden is most likely dead because the suspected terrorist has been unable to get treatment for his kidney disease..... Rumsfeld noted there were dozens of conflicting intelligence reports each day and said most of them were wrong. Most of the reports are based on sightings by local Afghans that cannot be verified." *CNN News*

"Reports today indicate that the government of Saudi Arabia is growing uncomfortable with the U.S. military presence in its country and may soon call for a U.S. withdrawal. But Secretary of State Colin Powell said today the Bush administration has not discussed that possibility with Saudi Arabia." *Cato Institute*

"But my mouth would encourage you; comfort from my lips would bring you relief." *Job 16:5 (NIV)*

Martin Luther King Day has just passed. He once stated, "The Negro needs the white man to free him from his fears. The white man needs the Negro to free him from his guilt. A doctrine of black supremacy is as evil as a doctrine of white supremacy."

Martin Luther King understood the fact we as a people, like those who gathered to help following the events of 9/11, needed to work together and put aside any differences. Those who offered their help never considered the victim's race, job, age or even their abilities. Portrayed was a time of helping and encouraging one another.

- **E**ncouragement is something you and I can offer one another.

- **N**urture comes from the words of each sister and brother.

- **C**omfort is found when we take the time to bother.

- **O**pportunity comes before us in many ways.

- **U**nity becomes a part of our passing days.

- **R**ewards for individual kind acts – that stays.

- **A**ccomplishments have been made that affect many.

- **G**ifts of personal love and support have been plenty.

- **E**ternal Blessing has been gently passed from many.

William Arthur Ward said, "Flatter me, and I may not believe you. Criticize me, and I may not like you. Ignore me, and I may not forgive you. Encourage me, and I will not forget you."

Prayer: Heavenly Father, we once again thank you for the many who offered their time, talents and treasures to help during the recovery efforts after 9/11. There was encouragement oozing on every corner and hope flowing in individual eyes. Encourage us to be true Soldiers of Christ who continually offer encouragement to those whom we serve with humbleness for You. Amen.

S.T.R.E.N.G.T.H.E.N. One Another

Jan 19: Article: "In Offices Near Ground Zero, Workers Gaze or Avert Eyes." "In the four months since two hijacked airplanes leveled the World Trade Center, there has been much action and debate at the disaster site. A viewing platform has been built to accommodate the crowds. Elaborate ideas have been proposed for formal memorials. And a million tons of debris have been removed as Lower Manhattan claws its way toward renewal." *by David W. Chen,*

"Casting the whole of your care [all your anxieties, all your worries, all your concerns, once and for all] on Him, for He cares for you affectionately and cares about you watchfully." *1 Peter 5:7 Amplified Bible*

"The happiest people I know are the ones who have learned how to hold everything loosely and have given the worrisome, stress-filled, fearful details of their lives into God's keeping." *– Charles R. Swindoll*

"By everyone's account, the contracting companies excavating the tons of broken steel and smoking debris at ground zero have worked with energy and devotion. But there is one thing they have worked without – insurance.

In one of the quiet subplots of the cleanup, the giant contractors that run the cranes and trucks and work crews at the World Trade Center site have been denied the basic liability coverage against injury and property damage that builders typically carry on every project, even on a single-family house.

Insurance companies, it turns out, have simply declined to provide the extensive coverage needed, believing that the cleanup project is too big and the risk too hard to measure. The companies, while providing one tiny policy, have also denied the city the broad insurance it sought to protect itself against potential lawsuits from people who believe they were sickened or injured by the mess at ground zero in Lower Manhattan.

And so for four months, a work site that has been called the most dangerous in the nation has been worked, quite incongruously, with virtually no insurance protection and thus some anxiously crossed fingers." – *Steven Greenhouse (NY Times)*

The laborers volunteered with uncertain support and apparently not a whole lot of assurance about coverage in case of needs; working and supporting one another with the inner strength of their convictions.

God's desire is that we learn, not to rely on ourselves only, but to find a new, ongoing, reviving strength which He will gladly provide during all the dark moments of our life. Look at the strength He provides.

- **S**orrow relieved – "My soul is weary with sorrow; strengthen me ..." *Psalm 119:28*

- **T**ears allowed – "My eyes pour out tears to God." *Job 16:20 NIV*

- **R**equest [Godly, not worldly request] honored - "Ask and it will be given to you." *Matthew 7:7*

- **E**strangements healed – "this son of mine was lost and is found!" *Luke 15:24 NIV*

- **N**othing refused – "All have sinned and come short of the Glory of God." *Romans 3:26 NIV*

- **G**race offered – "When you were dead in sin, ….God made you alive with Christ, He forgave us all or sins," *Colossians 2:13 NIV*

- **T**ruth presented – "I tell you, do not worry about your life." *Matthew 6:25 NIV*

- **H**ope instilled – "blessed are those who trust in the Lord and have made the Lord their hope and confidence." *Jeremiah 17:7 NIV*

- **E**ncouragement received – "...receive blessing...and vindication from ... their Savior. *Psalm 24:5 NIV*

- **N**ew life opportunity provided – "...we too may live a new life." *Romans 6:4 NIV*

Prayer: Lord, we thank You for the many ways you strengthen us as we live our daily life. Lead us to practice the fullness of Your Holy Words: "... be content with who you are, and don't put on airs. God's strong hand is on you; He'll promote you at the right time. Live carefree before God; he is most careful with you." *(1 Peter 5:6-7MSG)* Amen.

<u>O.N.E. By One</u>

Jan 21: "A member of Yasser Arafat's Fatah fires his gun into the air as he protests along with about 2,000 Palestinians Sunday in Gaza against Israeli military actions in the West Bank. After nearly a month of relative calm, the past week has seen a renewal of the retaliatory violence that has marked the conflict, now almost 16 months old." *LJWorld.com*

Jan23: "Wall Street Journal Reporter Daniel Pearl is Abducted in Karachi by Suspected Islamic Militants on January 23, 2002"

September11news.com

Discussion was quantitative and ongoing for the next couple nights concerning the news and the abducted reporter. Soldier's had their own theories about how they would escape, and many felt they were trained well enough to face the challenge. Others, in a more realistic manner, admitted how they would fear a situation like this and would hope someone would come to their rescue. Still others would not speculate about events overseas but simply wanted to deal with the present challenge in front of them.

Personally, I have learned to live a daily existence in God's presence and continually ask His help to face the challenges of the day no matter my location.

Scriptures tell us: "They went by night and surrounded the city. When the servant of the man of God got up and went out early the next morning, an army with horses and chariots had surrounded the city. 'Oh no, my Lord! What shall we do?' the servant asked. 'Don't be afraid,' the prophet answered. 'Those who are with us are more than those who are with them.' And Elisha prayed, 'Open his eyes, LORD, so that he may see.' Then the LORD opened the servant's eyes, and he looked and saw the hills full of horses and chariots of fire all around Elisha." *2 Kings 6:14b-17 (NIV)*

One of my grandson's favorite TV shows at the age of 3 was Wonder Pets. He would sing along with them and put emphasis on the part where they ask and answer the question, "what do we need." He would sing proudly and loudly "Teamwork!"

While in service following the events of 9/11, I saw a great deal of achievements completed one-by-one, but much more was the abundant amount of teamwork utilized to accomplish this difficult mission.

At this point in his life, the reporter Daniel Pearl physically stood alone. Not a place he wanted to be and no doubt a place most of us have no desire to be.

- **O**ne by one each day, each event, each service member's task continues until all is done.

- **N**otice how difficult it would be if you or I were designated to be the only one

- **E**ntreated alone to answer the call to serve, sacrifice, and struggle would not be fun.

"Randy Frazee has written a book called *The Connecting Church*. He has a son who was born without a left hand. One day in Sunday School the teacher was talking with the children about the church. To illustrate her point, she folded her hands together and said, "Here's the church, here's the steeple; open the doors and see all the people."

She asked the class to do it along with her – obviously not thinking about Randy's son's inability to pull this exercise off. Then it dawned on her that the boy wouldn't be able to join in.

Before she could do anything about it, the little boy next to his son, a friend of his from the time they were babies, reached out his left hand and said, "Let's do it together." The two boys proceeded to join their hands together to make the church and the steeple."

Frazee says, "This hand exercise should never be done again by an individual because the church is not a collection of individuals, but the one body of Christ."

The U.S. Army used to run a commercial that said they were an Army of One; I always had a problem with that commercial. Having spent several years in military service (40+) there were very few things one person could do alone. I might do an individual task, but those tasks often had to be coordinated with another person to complete the whole of the project or mission.

Prayer: Lord, I recognize that "one" is an important number to you, because each one of us is so special in Your sight. I am also reminded in Your word "...I say to you that if two of you agree on earth concerning anything that they ask, it will be done for them, by My Father in heaven. For where two or three are gathered together in My name, I am there in the midst of them." *(Matthew 18:19-21 NKJV)* It is true; our individual life is important in our relationship with the Father and sometimes very necessary. However, we are created to have fellowship with each other in our lives and our work. Instruct us on how to work together, one beside one to accomplish every situation You may place us in knowing You are there with us. Amen.

A.N.O.T.H.E.R. Opportunity

Jan 25: "Ashtabula, Ohio, and surrounding communities were shaken by a 4.5-magnitude earthquake at 10:03 p.m. eastern time on Thursday, January 25, 2001. This event followed a 2.6-magnitude earthquake on January 19, at 9:05 p.m. eastern time. The larger event was felt throughout an extensive area of northern Ohio, western Pennsylvania, Michigan, and Ontario, Canada. Preliminary damage reports from Ashtabula indicate cracked plaster and masonry, walls bowed or moved, items knocked off shelves, and a ruptured natural gas line that resulted in evacuation of some residents. Damage and felt reports are being gathered by the Division of Geological Survey, the U.S.

Geological Survey, and the Ashtabula County Emergency Management Agency." *(Ohio.gov)*

"Therefore, since we are surrounded by such a great cloud of witnesses, let us throw off everything that hinders and the sin that so easily entangles. And let us run with perseverance the race marked out for us, fixing our eyes on Jesus, the pioneer and perfecter of faith. For the joy set before him, he endured the cross, scorning its shame, and sat down at the right hand of the throne of God. Consider him who endured such opposition from sinners, so that you will not grow weary and lose heart." *Hebrews 12:1-3 (NIV)*

Things have settled, work continues at a steady rate. The military personnel continue to serve facing ongoing opportunities and challenges. We face another chance, another day, and another person. All are reminders that God has a plan which you and I are part of it.

- **A**nnounce to all who come your way

- **N**ever are we alone – even when we stray.

- **O**thers are there to provide support for challenging needs.

- **T**rust God's presence for you, in one form or another.

- **H**earing, helping, holding, as we sincerely pray.

- **E**ntrusting His angels to abide as He gently heeds.

- **R**eaching out His arms to show He cares – not to smother.

Prayer: Lord, once again we give thanks for those You bring into our lives, asking You to help us appreciate each and every person, knowing You allow our place in life for a purpose. Although we may not always know that purpose, may we recognize that we are never alone! For that fact and privilege we give You honor, praise and glory. Let Your Presence be known and shown through each of us. Thank You Lord! Amen.

A.M.E.N.

"Amen"

Feb 2: "Finland PM Lipponen Visits Ground Zero" *september11 news.com*

Feb 3: "WTC Flag at Super Bowl" september11news.com

Feb 8: "WTC Flag at Olympic Opening. Messages and Bears Left at WTC Review Stand." *september11news.com*

"I am the Alpha and the Omega," says the Lord God, "who is, and who was, and who is to come, the Almighty." *Revelations 1:8 NIV*

President George Washington said, "At disappointments and losses which are the effects of Providential acts, I never repine, because I am sure the divine disposer of events knows better than we do what is best for us, or what we deserve."

President Bush, in the 2002 State of the Union, stated:. "During these last few months, I've been humbled and privileged to see the true character of this country in a time of testing. Our enemies believed America was weak and materialistic, that we would splinter in fear and selfishness. The American people have responded magnificently, with courage and compassion, strength and resolve. As I have met the heroes, hugged the families and looked into the tired faces of rescuers, I have stood in awe of the American people."

- **A** great loss was experienced on 9/11 which was felt throughout the United States.

- **M**en and women came from all over to help New York City, for country members' sakes.

- **E**ach offered themselves with completeness, trying to relate

- **N**ow know their efforts did much to start a new developing state.

Thomas Jefferson once prayed: "Almighty God, who has given us this good land for our heritage, we humbly beseech Thee that we may always prove ourselves a people mindful of Thy favor and glad to do Thy will. Bless our land with honorable ministry, sound learning, and pure manners. Save us from violence, discord, and confusion, from pride and arrogance, and from every evil way. Defend our liberties, and fashion into one united people the multitude brought hither out of many kindred and tongues, all of which we ask through Jesus Christ our Lord, Amen."

Prayer: Heavenly Father, as we draw to a close my initial time at the site of the 9/11 attacks, I recognize You as the great Alpha and Omega and come to understand the words of **A. W. Tozer**, who stated: "In God there is no was or will be, but a continuous and unbroken is. In Him, history and prophecy are one and the same." Praise the Lord! Amen.

Chapter 15

The Journey to New Beginnings (87-90)

"The News, Enemies, Changes and Dreams continue."

April 1, 2002

"We have been recipients of the choicest bounties of Heaven. We have been preserved these many years, in peace and prosperity. We have grown in numbers, wealth and power as no other nation has ever grown; but we have forgotten God. Intoxicated with unbroken success, the necessity of redeeming and preserving grace, too proud to pray to the God that made us. It behooves us, then to humble ourselves before the offended Power to confess our national sins and to pray for clemency and forgiveness."

Abraham Lincoln, Proclamation of a National Day of Fasting and Prayer, March 30, 1863, Washington, D.C.

The N.E.W.S. Continues

"The house of the Lord [and His presence] shall be my dwelling place."
Psalm 23:6b AMP

"1 April 2002 –President and Mrs. Bush Host Easter Egg Roll on The South Lawn – 9:15 A.M.

"Today we have beautiful weather, and we hope you have a great time here at the traditional Easter Egg Roll" President Bush remarked." *georgewbush-whitehouse.archives.gov/news*

"**April 1, 2002**, President George W. Bush, Governor Pataki, and Mayor Bloomberg announced that the United States would sell Governors Island to the people of New York for a nominal cost, and that the island would be used for public benefit." *govisland.com*

"Press Secretary stated: For the first time in history, the Allies invoked NATO's collective defense commitment in the wake of the September 11 attacks. Since then, NATO Allies and many Partnership for Peace nations have contributed their military forces to Operation Enduring Freedom and offered blanket use of their airspace, ports and airfields. This cooperation underscores the trans-Atlantic commitment to shared values and collective defense that NATO has embodied for over fifty years." *georgewbush-whitehouse.archives.gov*

"Jesus Christ (the Messiah) is [always] the same, yesterday, today, [yes] and forever (to the ages). Do not be carried about by different and varied and alien teachings; for it is good for the heart to be established and ennobled and strengthened by means of grace (God's favor and spiritual blessing)" *Hebrews 13:8-9a AMP*

- Nowhere do we find the character of God has changed.

- Everywhere we look the world is continually changing.

- Why not connect with the One whose plan has been arranged.

- Seek His presence and let Him do the arranging.

On April 1st I reported to a new assignment within the city, where I have been assigned to an armory. There I received a new set of living quarters at an inner city apartment home for priests, where I met others doing their work for God. My assignment was to do some fill-in for Chaplains who have remained throughout the Easter season and those Chaplains who had been activated with their units; who were now preparing to head overseas for a tour of duty.

I saw life had boldly moved on, while in some areas it remained stagnant. We celebrated the Easter Egg hunt, with the nation as an annual event, while advancing decisions about the future of our service member's roll within the city.

The news of our responsibilities within the city continued. Sometimes the news was good and sometimes not so good. The news of God continues faithfully, with news of hope and victory mixed with challenge and frustration, leading to an inheritance that will last a lifetime.

Prayer: Some days, Lord, I fear turning to the news because I fear what has happened. We live in a troubled world of humanity struggling to find peace. Lord, if they only knew or if we would only tell them that there is a place of peace. It is a wonderful place, Lord, and You are there with me and so many others. Give us the strength and desire to lead others to find Jesus and become bathed in that "peace that passes understanding" (Philippians 4:7) which comes only from You. Amen.

Our E.N.E.M.I.E.S. Continue

"2 April 2002 – Statement by the Press Secretary – We believe that one of the individuals captured by Pakistani authorities in recent raids is Abu Zubaydah, who is a key terrorist recruiter, an operational planner, and a member of Osama bin Laden's inner circle." *georgewbush-whitehouse.archives.gov*

"3 April 2002 – *President at Fisher for Governor Reception – Four Seasons Hotel – Philadelphia, Pennsylvania.* "I wake up every morning and I get into the great, beautiful Oval Office, and I read a threat assessment. It reminds me that we're still threatened. But I'm here to tell you, our country is responding. We're diligent, we're alert. We know our mission, and we know our priority. But the best way to defend the homeland, the best way to make sure our little ones can grow up in a peaceful world, is to find the enemy, wherever they try to hide, and bring them to justice." *georgewbush-whitehouse.archives.gov*

"Now Ahimaaz son of Zadok said, 'Let me run and take the news to the king that the LORD has vindicated him by delivering him from the hand of his enemies.' 'You are not the one to take the news today,' Joab told him. 'You may take the news another time, but you must not do so today, because the king's son is dead.' *2 Samuel 18:19-20 NIV*

Enemies remain a strong part of our lives including the enemies hidden in the shadows of our lives. How we face them is a personal choice:

- Everywhere I look within the city, I see life has moved on since the great tragedy.

- Notice how the pace of life has become more rapid and less involved with the individual.

- Every once in a while, someone on the street will comment on how they still hurt badly.

- Most of the remembrances and struggles remain where you see trucks loaded with stuff to haul.

- Individual memorials, teddy bear walls, never-ending pictures are looking ever so sadly.

- Each person who is cleaning, guarding, supervising and providing is still reminded of it all.

- Since 9/11, life has moved on; however, many still struggle with their internal, indecisive, individual shadow of death tragedy.

Remarks by Dr. Rice at the 2002 National Commemoration of the Days of Remembrance – U.S. Capitol Rotunda – Washington, D.C. – "We gather today to remember that evil is real and present in our world. We gather to remember that hatred and bigotry are always and everywhere wrong. We gather to remember that the commission of monstrous sin requires not our consent, but only our indifference, our neutrality, or our silence. We gather to light six candles, so that we may never forget six million acts of murder.

With each passing year, the number of living Holocaust survivors and liberators grows smaller. When all the eyewitnesses are gone, the Holocaust's history will be taught not from the searing pain of memory but from the pressing call of conscience." *10 April 2002 georgewbush-whitehouse.archives.gov*

On March 31, 2002 the Christian church celebrated Easter. The enemy of Christ considered himself victorious a short time before. However, Praise the Lord, he was proven so wrong, as Christ walked through the shadow and beat our greatest enemy – death. You and I have been vindicated by the Son of our Heavenly Host who was dead and is now very much alive.

Prayer: Heavenly Father, we know we face enemies in our existence. Some are very present and some are memories from the past. We know that sometimes we are our own worst enemy. Lead us to receive the news and find the victory of knowing that our greatest enemy – death – has been defeated. We can rejoice. Amen.

C.H.A.N.G.E.S. Continue

"April 8, 2002 – President Emphasizes Message to Middle East – Remarks by the President to the Press Pool Following Tour of the Citizens Police Academy Knoxville, Tennessee 12:06 P.M. EDT

"Let me say one thing before I leave. First of all, I meant what I said to the Prime Minister of Israel. I expect there to be withdrawal without delay. And I also meant what I said to the Arab world, that in order for there to be peace, nations must stand up, leaders must stand up and condemn terrorism, terrorist activity.

There is a mutual responsibility to achieve peace, and it's going to require leadership on both sides. And the United States is firmly committed to achieving peace, and is firmly committed – I am firmly committed, to what I expect from both parties.

I repeat, I meant what I said about withdrawal without delay, and I mean what I say when I call upon the Arab world to strongly condemn and act against terrorist activity." *georgewbush-whitehouseArchives .gov*

"9 Apr 2002 – On National Former Prisoner of War Recognition Day, we recognize the sacrifice of our former POWs and remember with honor their heroism. We also pledge that we will work to ensure that future generations will understand and appreciate the courage and contributions of these selfless heroes.

NOW, THEREFORE, I, GEORGE W. BUSH, President of the United States of America, by virtue of the authority vested in me by the Constitution and laws of the United States, do hereby proclaim April 9, 2002, as National Former Prisoner of War Recognition Day. *georgewbush-whitehouse.archives.gov*

Change is inevitable and we all must face it. Some changes we can accept, whereas other changes we may need to evaluate and make changes within ourselves. "Am I now trying to win the approval of men, or of God? Or am I trying to please men? If I were still trying to please men, I would not be a servant of Christ." (Galatians 1:10. NIV) Let us be willing to recognize who we are, and answer the question of this passage.

One answer to enable us to change came from an example in the life Jesus described in His Holy Word.

'Jesus called over a child, whom he stood in the middle of the room, and said, "I'm telling you, once and for all, that unless you return to square one and start over like children, you're not even going to get a look at the kingdom, let alone get in. Whoever becomes simple and elemental again, like this child, will rank high in God's kingdom. What's more, when you receive the childlike on my account, it's the same as receiving me." (*Matthew 8:2-5*)

- Change is something we hesitate,

- Harboring fears deep within.

- Anticipating the negative we relate,

- Never ready to honestly begin.

- Go ahead and open a new gate,

- Enter in – take a chance – you will win!

- Since God is in charge – let's not hesitate

Changes are common ingredients in a service member's life. We have certain routines, but we know that somewhere, sometime, we will be expected to go somewhere or do something that is totally different from anything we have done before. We may be trained, experienced, and we may have taught others. Then something new slips in that were not expecting, and we have to start all over again, learning a new way to accomplish what we have done many times before.

President Bush in his State of the Union address continued: "We'll be deliberate, yet time is not on our side. I will not wait on events while dangers gather. I will not stand by as peril draws closer and closer. The United States of America will not permit the world's most dangerous regimes to threaten us with the world's most destructive weapons.

Our war on terror is well begun, but it is only begun. This campaign may not be finished on our watch, yet it must be and it will be waged on our watch." *georgewbush-whitehouse.archives.gov*

Our walk with God is no different but much simpler. We make it too difficult. God wants a simple, trusting, accepting faith walk with Him. Not the analytical, theological, eschatological walk – just a simple one.

- "Ask and you shall receive, seek and you shall find, knock and the door shall be opened unto you (and me)." *Matthew 7:7NIV*

- "Do all things without grumbling or disputing." *Philippians 2:14*

Prayer: Heavenly Father, the words of Scriptures sound easy enough. However, I try to reason and understand rather than accept and trust. Help me see the simplicity of walking with and trusting in You. Amen.

Our D.R.E.A.M.S. Continue

"April 4, 2002 – Today, as we mark the 34th anniversary of the assassination of Dr. Martin Luther King, Jr., I join my fellow Americans in remembering Dr. King and renewing his call for equality and justice for all our citizens." *gpo.gov*

"Dr. King was a man of deep faith who dedicated his life to a crucial and just cause that changed this Nation. He graciously and peacefully called for our country to abide by the principles of unity, equality, and racial justice for every citizen regardless of race, creed, or background. For too brief a time, our Nation benefited from his work, yet his dream lives on in the hearts of a new generation. I join all citizens in recognizing this important American and his legacy of freedom, equality, and justice for all." — George W. Bush *gpo.gov*

Martin Luther King had a dream that cost him his life. Over the years I have met many focused people and too many unfocused people during my travels in ministries both within the military and the local church. As I come to the close of this historical, personal and spiritual journey through my time following the events of 9/11 and the shadow of death, I encourage each of you to consider the simple D.R.E.A.M. listed, in the sentence, below by applying it to the scriptures, your life and your walk with God.

*Do **Right** Enter Another Mission Serving.*

As I was walking back to my room at the end of a long day of Critical Incident Stress Debriefings (CISD) I noticed 3 circling lights in the sky over the armory. They puzzled me. Were we being visited by aliens? Were they helicopters circling the area? I heard no sound, and the lights seemed very close together. Or maybe, because I was so tired, I was just dreaming – I do not know.

"Brothers and sisters, I do not consider myself yet to have taken hold of it. But one thing I do: Forgetting what is behind and straining toward what is ahead, I press on toward the goal to win the prize for which God has called me heavenward in Christ Jesus." *Philippians 3:13-14 NIV*

I repeat: *Do **Right** Enter Another Mission Serving.*

"All of us, then, who are mature should take such a view of things. And if on some point you think differently, that too God will make clear to you." *Philippians 3:15 NIV*

"First came the atom bomb, the stealth bomber and the airborne laser. Now comes the US military's latest fearsome weapon: the indestructible sandwich.

Capable of surviving airdrops, rough handling and extreme climates, and just about anything except a GI's jaws, the new "pocket" sandwich is designed to stay "fresh" for up to three years at 26 °C (about the temperature of a warm summer's day), or for six months at 38 °C (just over body temperature).

Soldiers who tried the pepperoni and barbecue-chicken pocket sandwiches have found them 'acceptable.' They are now planning to extend the menu to pocket pizzas, as well as cream-filled bagels, breakfast burritos and even peanut-butter sandwiches. Like dehydrated egg, freeze-dried coffee and processed cheese – all originally developed by the military – the long-life sandwich will probably find its way into grocery stores." *Talk about a dream: US military creates indestructible sandwich - 10 April 2002 by Duncan Graham-Rowe*

Prayer: Dear Father, Son and Holy Spirit we are not indestructible, but we can dream. I am so grateful for Your Presence in all areas of the lives of those who believe and even those who do not. Help us recognize your thoughts from Jeremiah because they are available to each one of us: "I know the plans I have for you," declares the LORD, "plans to prosper you and not to harm you, plans to give you hope and a future." (Jeremiah 29:11 NIV). I rejoice that You have plans for us and ask that You will guide all who ask to develop a personal dream that matches Your Divine Plan. Thank you Lord. Amen.

Epilogue

"In the sacrifice of soldiers, the fierce brotherhood of firefighters, and the bravery and generosity of ordinary citizens, we have glimpsed what a new culture of responsibility could look like. We want to be a nation that serves goals larger than self. We have been offered a unique opportunity, and we must not let this moment pass." Those of us who have lived through these challenging times have been changed by them. We've come to know truths that we will never question: Evil is real, and it must be opposed. Steadfast in our purpose, we now press on. We have known freedom's price. We have shown freedom's power. And in this great conflict, my fellow Americans, we will see freedom's victory." *President, George W. Bush, State of the Union Address, 29 January 2002*

2 May 2011: The news came that many had wanted to hear since the events of 9/11 occurred – Bin Laden is dead. *The Christian Science Monitor* tells us: "Pakistan army soldiers seen near the house where it is believed al-Qaeda leader Osama bin Laden lived in Abbottabad, Pakistan on Monday, May 2. Bin Laden, the mastermind behind the Sept. 11, 2001, terror attacks that killed thousands of people, was slain in his hideout in Pakistan early Monday in a firefight with U.S. forces, ending a manhunt that spanned a frustrating decade." And the world celebrated – especially in New York City. Closure occurred for many, healing for others. However, it was also a deadening reminder for those still grieving in the shadows of despair.

Glen Beck made an interesting statement; "Celebrate today, roll up your sleeves tomorrow, for the job is not done."

Today, as I concluded my journal-devotional, my heart was stirred. I do not know if it is with delight or sorrow: delight from the news of the day or sorrow as I remember the loss from an event that brought about this time of celebration and the possibility of another soul lost to eternity's rewards.

However, our personal journey through The Valley of the Shadow of Death continues, as we live each day knowing that every day brings us closer to our own death, "…about that day or hour no one knows, not even the angels in heaven, nor the Son, but only the Father" (Matthew 24:36 *NIV)*. My time within the city has been completed. I bid farewell to all those precious individuals who provided support, food, comfort, and to those who worked the many hours in search and recovery, medical and perimeter support. May God help us remember how this tragedy united a people to accomplish God's work in many different avenues?

Personally, I am ready to "dwell in the house of the Lord forever" (Psalm 23:6b NKJV), and my prayer is that all who read these pages will know when you face **The Shadow of Death**, you have nothing to fear if you are ready – Praise the Lord!

Prayer: "I have seen the burden God has laid on the human race. He has made everything beautiful in its time. He has also set eternity in the human heart, yet no one can fathom what God has done from beginning to end. I know that there is nothing better for people than to be happy and to do good while they live." *Ecclesiastes 3:10-12 NIV* Amen and Amen.

ABOUT THE AUTHOR

Chaplain (LTC) Patrick L. Holder (retired) is married to Betty V. (West). They are the parents of 2 grown daughters – Joy and Melissa. He served student pastorates while attending Bible School at Elim Bible Institute in Lima, NY; college at William Jennings Bryan in Dayton, Tennessee; and Asbury Theological Seminary in Wilmore Kentucky. He also served in 4 churches, within the Upper New York State United Methodist Conference, after leaving active military continuing to remain in Active Reserves then the National Guard.

Chaplain Holder's military service spans from January 26, 1966 until March 17, 2006. He completed 10 years of enlisted, active and reserve, with a tour as a Chaplain Assistant/Medic in Viet Nam (1966-67). He also served as Elim Fellowship's, first Army chaplain, from 1976 until his retirement. This included additional active duty time with a tours during Desert Storm in 1991 and a NY Guard call-up for 9/11. His complete military history may be found at www.withyoualways.net.

CPSIA information can be obtained at www.ICGtesting.com
Printed in the USA
BVOW020122071111

275430BV00002B/3/P